TRAVELLERS' VERSE

NEW EXCURSIONS INTO ENGLISH POETRY

EDITORS: W. J. TURNER AND SHEILA SHANNON

TRAVELLERS' VERSE

CHOSEN BY M. G. LLOYD THOMAS

WITH

ORIGINAL LITHOGRAPHS

BY

EDWARD BAWDEN

> *Sometimes o'er distant climes I stray,*
> *By guides experienced taught the way;*
> *The wonders of each region view,*
> *From frozen Lapland to Peru;*
> *Bound o'er rough seas, and mountains bare,*
> *Yet ne'er forsake my elbow chair . . .*
>
> —SOAME JENYNS

LONDON
FREDERICK MULLER LTD
29 Great James Street
WC I

FIRST PUBLISHED BY FREDERICK MULLER LTD
IN 1946

PRINTED IN GREAT BRITAIN
AT THE CURWEN PRESS
PLAISTOW E13

PRODUCED BY ADPRINT LIMITED

GUIDE

IN *The Anatomy of Melancholy* Burton recalls the effects of travel on one who went voyaging after he had made an end of his tedious wars:

> 'He took great content, exceeding delight in that his voyage, as who doth not that shall attempt the like . . .? For peregrination charms our senses with such unspeakable and sweet variety, that some count him unhappy that never travelled, a kinde of prisoner, and pity his case, that from his cradle to his old age beholds the same still; still, still the same, the same!'

The feelings which Burton describes here are recognizable enough, and anyone who does not dislike verse and who is familiar with such feelings may be interested to read about travel as poets have experienced it.

Travellers' Verse is verse by those who have travelled in fancy or in fact, or in both. Some poets write from the spot—Prior from the Hague, Ambrose Philips from Copenhagen, Lady Mary Wortley Montagu from Pera, 'Monk' Lewis from sea within ten days' sail of Antigua—and so on. Others might agree with John Scott of Amwell that 'He who describes what he has seen, may describe correctly: he, who describes what he has not seen, must depend for much on the accounts of others, and supply the rest from his own imagination.' *Travellers' Verse* is intended for the reader whose travels may or may not have taken him across actual seas, but who, when he makes journeys in his mind, can adapt himself easily; it is meant for him who feels no more than the proper amount of alarm if, having bidden farewell to the Tagus on departing with Sir Thomas Wyatt for London, he is immediately required to sail instead with Don Juan for Leghorn. Don Juan will get shipwrecked, but it is hoped that the reader himself will not refuse on that account to disembark at Leghorn where he will find Shelley composing a letter to Maria Gisborne.

Later on, having visited Egypt, he will be asked to sail tropical seas in the company of Mr. Belloc's Commander Sin, and then, as if for the first time, to reach Africa. In such a casual fashion and by routes often more unorthodox than this he will get conducted round the world. He will leave many countries but no continent unvisited. His guide will sometimes be one of the great poets, sometimes an accomplished versifier or a lesser poet. The reader will look through the eyes of any century from the sixteenth to the twentieth, and the character of the writing is correspondingly diverse.

An anthology of this kind needs variety, but the variety here may be thought, for so short a book, excessive. There is some peril in passing from words and rhythms used by Spenser or by Yeats for the communication of their vision of life to the flaccid vocabulary and versification of John Kenyon, whose *Travelled Oyster* has seemed, all the same, amusing enough to include. The perils of solemnity are probably much greater. It is the sequence in which the poems are arranged that should make such transitions seem unviolent, unless, as sometimes, incompatible passages are deliberately arranged in such a way as to produce the shock of contrast. It is not likely that the intricacies of arrangement have always been happily contrived, but it is even less likely that the reader is going to be bound by any compiler's order: he makes his own as he pleases.

This choice of poems, in its irresponsible fashion embracing the world, might have been restricted to the poetry of a single age, and even so have had to be selected from too generous an amount of material. Again, accounts of the foolish traveller through the ages would be as hard to compress into a book the size of this. Innumerable passages in Elizabethan literature alone are directed against the French, Spanish or 'Italianate' affectations acquired by the English traveller, and depictions of the foolish traveller did not end with the Elizabethans; as a literary butt he has never been out of fashion. In the eighteenth century we hear often enough of the 'Modern Fine Gentleman' returned from the Grand Tour—'A monster of such complicated worth, That no one single clime could e'er bring forth'. Probably none but a character in prose fiction, that 'Prince of the Almighty's creation' Sir Charles Grandison, could be relied upon at that time to reap only the benefits of foreign travel. As Harriet Byron writes to Lucy Selby:

'Travelling! Young men travelling! I cannot, my dear, but think it a very nonsensical thing! . . .
'To see a parcel of giddy boys under the direction of tutors or governors hunting after—What?—Nothing; or at best but ruins of ruins . . .

'And when this *grand tour* is completed, the travelled youth returns: And, what is his boast? Why, to be able to tell, perhaps his *better*-taught friend, who has never been out of his native country, what the other has a juster idea of from reading; and of which, it is more than probable, he can give a much better account than the traveller.

'"And are these, petulant Harriet" (methinks, Lucy, you demand) "all the benefits that you will suppose Sir Charles Grandison has reaped from his travelling?"

'Why no. But then, in my turn, I ask, Is every traveller, a Sir Charles Grandison?'

Countries, too, have been arbitrarily treated. Italy is poets' country. For that reason more space is given to it than for example to Russia. Then, to an anthologist of travellers' verse, English poets seem to have been sometimes almost obsessed by the Middle East—by deserts and camels. Not all these camels have as much life as the 'foolish' and 'great-spleen'd' in one of Chapman's similes. Many of the deserts are as arid as might be feared and their camels as intractable. When that has been allowed for the camel has still had to be restrained from dominating the book.

The only general rules which have been observed are that no one author shall appear very frequently or at very great length— a rule often harsh in the application, to Byron especially—and that translation shall not be admitted. (Mr. Colum's piece about lehua trees 'imitates but does not translate an Hawaiian poem', but James Elroy Flecker's *Lord Arnaldos* has been quite inconsistently allowed.)

The compass and the theme of the book have precluded any attempt to choose what is 'representative' of countries or of poets. The selection may accidentally represent a given writer fairly; it is much more likely that it does not. Some countries have been ignored because they are not on any of the routes adopted in the anthology. Sometimes countries that are on the route—Belgium, for instance—are traversed in silence because a hundred and eighteen pages cannot be made to include all stages of so erratic a journey round the world. No attempt has been made to do justice to the poetry of America or to that of the Dominions. The choice has been difficult enough as it is; the English poets are not an insular people.

I wish to thank the General Editors for valuable suggestions, as well as for the idea of compiling an anthology of poems about travel. To Edward Bawden I owe a great debt for his illustrations. Those friends who have allowed their talents and goodwill to be exploited, but whose names are not given here, are aware, I hope, of my appreciation. Acknowledgements to authors and publishers are made in the notes.

The only thanks that I could suitably offer to my sister Nesta would be in the form of a dedication. Direct dedications are not customary in the Series and for this reason alone she escapes.

October 1945   M.G.Ll.T.

TRAVELLERS' VERSE

THOMAS LOVE PEACOCK 1785–1866

1. FOR WHAT GOOD END?

Gryllus:

  I see long trains of strange machines on wheels,
  With one in front of each, puffing white smoke
  From a black, hollow column. Fast and far
  They speed, like yellow leaves before the gale,
  When autumn winds are strongest. Through their windows
  I judge them thronged with people; but distinctly
  Their speed forbids my seeing.

Spirit-Rapper: This is one
  Of the great glories of our modern time.
  'Men are become as birds,' and skim like swallows
  The surface of the world.

Gryllus: For what good end?

Spirit-Rapper:

  The end is in itself—the end of skimming
  The surface of the world.

THOMAS STEARNS ELIOT b. 1888

from

The Rock

2. LIKE ALL MEN IN ALL PLACES

  Like all men in all places,

  Some went from love of glory,
  Some went who were restless and curious,
  Some were rapacious and lustful.
  Many left their bodies to the kites of Syria
  Or sea-strewn along the routes;
  Many left their souls in Syria,

Living on, sunken in moral corruption;
Many came back well broken,
Diseased and beggared, finding
A stranger at the door in possession:
Came home cracked by the sun of the East
And the seven deadly sins in Syria.

EDMUND SPENSER C. 1552–1599

from

Complaints

3. TO WANDER TO THE WORLDS ENDE

Certes (said he) I meane me to disguize
In some straunge habit, after vncouth wize,
Or like a Pilgrime, or a Lymiter,
Or like a *Gipsen*, or a Iuggeler,
And so to wander to the worlds ende,
To seeke my fortune, where I may it mend
For worse than that I haue, I cannot meete.
Wide is the world I wote and euerie streete
Is full of fortunes, and aduentures straunge
Continuallie subiect vnto chaunge.

SAMUEL DANIEL C. 1563–1619

4. ULYSSES AND THE SIREN

Siren

Come worthy Greek, Ulysses, come
Possess these shores with me:
The winds and seas are troublesome,
And here we may be free
  Here may we sit, and view their toil
That travail in the deep,
And joy the day in mirth the while,
And spend the night in sleep.

2

Ulysses

Fair nymph, if fame or honour were
To be attained with ease,
Then would I come and rest me there,
And leave such toils as these.
But here it dwells, and here must I
With danger seek it forth:
To spend the time luxuriously
Becomes not men of worth.

Siren

Ulysses, O be not deceived
With that unreal name;
This honour is a thing conceived,
And rests on others' fame;
Begotten only to molest
Our peace, and to beguile
The best thing of our life, our rest,
And give us up to toil.

Ulysses

Delicious nymph, suppose there were
Nor honour, nor report,
Yet manliness would scorn to wear
The time in idle sport:
For toil doth give a better touch
To make us feel our joy;
And ease finds tediousness as much
As labour yields annoy.

Siren

Then pleasure likewise seems the shore,
Whereto tends all your toil,
Which you forgo to make it more,
And perish oft the while.
Who may disport them diversely
Find never tedious day,
And ease may have variety,
As well as action may.

Ulysses

But natures of the noblest frame
These toils and dangers please,
And they take comfort in the same,
As much as you in ease;
　And with the thought of actions past
Are recreated still;
When pleasure leaves a touch at last,
To shew that it was ill.

Siren

That doth opinion only cause
That's out of custom bred,
Which makes us many other laws
Than ever nature did.
　No widows wail for our delights,
Our sports are without blood;
The world we see by warlike wights
Receives more hurt than good.

Ulysses

But yet the state of things require
These motions of unrest,
And these great spirits of high desire
Seem born to turn them best;
　To purge the mischiefs that increase
And all good order mar:
For oft we see a wicked peace
To be well changed for war.

Siren

Well, well, Ulysses, then I see
I shall not have thee here,
And therefore I will come to thee,
And take my fortune there.
　I must be won that cannot win,
Yet lost were I not won:
For beauty hath created been
T'undo, or be undone.

5. LORD ARNALDOS

¿ Quien hubiese tal ventura ?

The strangest of adventures,
That happen by the sea,
Befell to Lord Arnaldos
On the Evening of St. John;
For he was out a-hunting—
A huntsman bold was he!—
When he beheld a little ship
And close to land was she.
Her cords were all of silver,
Her sails of cramasy;
And he who sailed the little ship
Was singing at the helm:
The waves stood still to hear him,
The wind was soft and low;
The fish who dwell in darkness
Ascended through the sea,
And all the birds in heaven
Flew down to his mast-tree.
Then spake the Lord Arnaldos,
(Well shall you hear his words!)
'Tell me for God's sake, sailor,
What song may that song be?'
The sailor spake in answer,
And answer thus made he:
'I only tell my song to those
Who sail away with me.'

from

Paradise Lost

6. THE GOODLY PROSPECT

Satan from hence now on the lower stair
That scal'd by steps of Gold to Heav'n Gate
Looks down with wonder at the sudden view
Of all this World at once. As when a Scout
Through dark and desart wayes with peril gone
All night; at last by break of chearful dawne
Obtains the brow of some high-climbing Hill,
Which to his eye discovers unaware
The goodly prospect of some forein land
First seen, or some renownd Metropolis
With glistering Spires and Pinnacles adornd,
Which now the Rising Sun guilds with his beams.

JOHN FORD 1586–c. 1640

from

Love's Sacrifice

7. PRAY INSTRUCT ME

Roseilli:

You are, my Lord Fernando, late return'd
From travels; pray instruct me, since the voice
Of most supreme authority commands
My absence: I determine to bestow
Some time in learning languages abroad;
Perhaps the change of air may change in me
Remembrance of my wrongs at home: good sir,
Inform me; say I meant to live in Spain,
What benefit of knowledge might I treasure?

Fernando:

    Troth, sir, I'll freely speak as I have found:
In Spain you lose experience; 'tis a climate
Too hot to nourish arts; the nation proud,
And in their pride unsociable; the court
More pliable to glorify itself
Than do a stranger grace: if you intend
To traffic like a merchant, 'twere a place
Might better much your trade; but as for me,
I soon took surfeit on it.

Roseilli: What for France?

Fernando:

    France I more praise and love. You are, my lord,
Yourself for horsemanship much fam'd; and there
You shall have many proofs to shew your skill.
The French are passing courtly, ripe of wit,
Kind, but extreme dissemblers; you shall have
A Frenchman ducking lower than your knee,
At th' instant mocking even your very shoe-ties:
To give the country due, it is on earth
A paradise; and if you can neglect
Your own appropriaments, but praising that
In others, wherein you excel yourself,
You shall be much belov'd there.

SAMUEL TAYLOR COLERIDGE 1772–1834

8. THE DELINQUENT TRAVELLERS

Some are home-sick—some two or three,
Their third year on the Arctic Sea—
Brave Captain Lyon tells us so—
Spite of those charming Esquimaux.
But O, what scores are sick of Home,
Agog for Paris or for Rome!
Nay! tho' contented to abide,
You should prefer your own fireside;

Yet since grim War has ceas'd its madding,
And Peace has set John Bull agadding,
'Twould such a vulgar taste betray,
For very shame you must away! . . .
Keep moving! Steam, or Gas, or Stage,
Hold, cabin, steerage, hencoop's cage—
Tour, Journey, Voyage, Lounge, Ride, Walk,
Skim, Sketch, Excursion, Travel-talk—
For move you must! 'Tis now the rage,
The law and fashion of the Age.
If you but perch, where Dover tallies,
So strangely with the coast of Calais,
With a good glass and knowing look,
You'll soon get matter for a book!
Or else, in Gas-car, take your chance
Like that adventurous king of France,
Who, once, with twenty thousand men
Went up—and then came down again;
At least, he moved if nothing more:
And if there's nought left to explore,
Yet while your well-greased wheels keep spinning,
The traveller's honoured name you're winning,
And, snug as Jonas in the Whale,
You may loll back and dream a tale.
Move, or be moved—there's no protection,
Our Mother Earth has ta'en the infection—
(That rogue Copernicus, 'tis said
First put the whirring in her head,)
A planet She, and can't endure
T'exist without her annual Tour. . . .
While streams and shopkeepers, we see,
Will have their run toward the sea—
And if, meantime, like old King Log,
Or ass with tether and a clog,
Must graze at home! to yawn and bray
'I guess we shall have rain to-day!'
Nor clog nor tether can be worse
Than the dead palsy of the purse.
Money, I've heard a wise man say,
Makes herself wings and flys away:

Ah! would She take it in her head
To make a pair for me instead!
At all events, the Fancy's free,
No traveller so bold as she.
From Fear and Poverty released
I'll saddle Pegasus, at least,
And when she's seated to her mind,
I within I can mount behind:
And since this outward I, you know,
Must stay because he cannot go,
My fellow-travellers shall be they
Who go, because they cannot stay—
Rogues, rascals, sharpers, blanks and prizes,
Delinquents of all sorts and sizes,
Fraudulent bankrupts, Knights burglarious,
And demireps of means precarious—
All whom Law thwarted, Arms or Arts,
Compel to visit foreign parts, . . .
But ere we cross the main once more,
Methinks, along my native shore,
Dismounting from my steed I'll stray
Beneath the cliffs of Dumpton Bay,
Where, Ramsgate and Broadstairs between,
Rude caves and grated doors are seen:
And here I'll watch till break of day,
(For Fancy in her magic might
Can turn broad noon to starless night!)
When lo! methinks a sudden band
Of smock-like smugglers round me stand.
Denials, oaths, in vain I try,
At once they gag me for a spy,
And stow me in the boat hard by.
Suppose us fairly now afloat,
Till Boulogne mouth receives our Boat.
But, bless us! what a numerous band
Of cockneys anglicise the strand!
Delinquent bankrupts, leg-bail'd debtors,
Some for the news, and some for letters—
With hungry look and tarnished dress,
French shrugs and British surliness.

Sick of the country for their sake
Of them and France *French leave* I take—
And lo! a transport comes in view
I hear the merry motley crew,
Well skill'd in pocket to make entry,
Of Dieman's Land the elected Gentry,
And founders of Australian Races.—
The Rogues! I see it in their faces!
Receive me, Lads! I'll go with you,
Hunt the black swan and kangaroo,
And that New Holland we'll presume
Old England with some elbow-room.
Across the mountains we will roam,
And each man make himself a home:
Or, if old habits ne'er forsaking,
Like clock-work of the Devil's making,
Ourselves inveterate rogues should be,
We'll have a virtuous progeny;
And on the dunghill of our vices
Raise human pine-apples and spices.
Of all the children of John Bull
With empty heads and bellies full,
Who ramble, East, West, North and South,
With leaky purse and open mouth,
In search of varieties exotic
The usefullest and most patriotic,
And merriest, too, believe me, Sirs!
Are your Delinquent Travellers!

from

The Two Gentlemen of Verona

9. ADIEU

Proteus:

Wilt thou be gone? Sweet Valentine, adieu!
Think on thy Proteus, when thou haply seest
Some rare note-worthy object in thy travel:
Wish me partaker in thy happiness,
When thou dost meet good hap; and in thy danger,
If ever danger do environ thee,
Commend thy grievance to my holy prayers,
For I will be thy beadsman, Valentine.

GEORGE GORDON LORD BYRON 1788–1824

from

Don Juan

10. ONE'S NATIVE LAND RECEDING

I can't but say it is an awkward sight
    To see one's native land receding through
The growing waters; it unmans one quite,
    Especially when life is rather new:
I recollect Great Britain's coast looks white,
    But almost every other country's blue,
When gazing on them, mystified by distance,
We enter on our nautical existence.

11. DOVER TO MUNICH

Farewell, farewell! Before our prow
  Leaps in white foam the noisy channel;
A tourist's cap is on my brow,
  My legs are cased in tourist's flannel:

Around me gasp the invalids—
  The quantity to-night is fearful—
I take a brace or so of weeds,
  And feel (as yet) extremely cheerful.

The night wears on:—my thirst I quench
  With one imperial pint of porter;
Then drop upon a casual bench—
  (The bench is short, but I am shorter)—

Place 'neath my head the *havre-sac*
  Which I have stowed my little all in,
And sleep, though moist about the back,
  Serenely in an old tarpaulin. . . .

Bed at Ostend at 5 a.m.
  Breakfast at 6, and train 6.30,
Tickets to Königswinter (mem.
  The seats unutterably dirty).

And onward thro' those dreary flats
  We move, with scanty space to sit on,
Flanked by stout girls with steeple hats,
  And waists that paralyse a Briton;—

By many a tidy little town,
  Where tidy little Fraus sit knitting;
(The men's pursuits are, lying down,
  Smoking perennial pipes, and spitting;)

And doze, and execrate the heat,
　And wonder how far off Cologne is,
And if we shall get aught to eat,
　Till we get there, save raw polonies:

Until at last the 'gray old pile'
　Is seen, is past, and three hours later
We're ordering steaks, and talking vile
　Mock-German to an Austrian waiter. . . .

On, on the vessel steals;
　Round go the paddle-wheels,
And now the tourist feels
　　As he should;
For king-like rolls the Rhine,
And the scenery's divine,
And the victuals and the wine
　　Rather good.

From every crag we pass'll
Rise up some hoar old castle;
The hanging fir-groves tassel
　　Every slope;
And the vine her lithe arms stretches
Over peasants singing catches—
And you'll make no end of sketches,
　　I should hope.

We've a nun here (called Thérèse),
Two couriers out of place,
One Yankee with a face
　　Like a ferret's:
And three youths in scarlet caps
Drinking chocolate and schnapps—
A diet which perhaps
　Has its merits.

And day again declines:
In shadow sleep the vines,
And the last ray thro' the pines
 Feebly glows,
Then sinks behind yon ridge;
And the usual evening midge
Is settling on the bridge
 Of my nose.

And keen's the air and cold,
And the sheep are in the fold,
And Night walks sable-stoled
 Thro' the trees;
And on the silent river
The floating starbeams quiver;—
And now, the saints deliver
 Us from fleas. . . .

Avenues of broad white houses,
 Basking in the noontide glare;—
Streets, which foot of traveller shrink from,
 As on hot plates shrinks the bear;—

Elsewhere lawns, and vista'd gardens,
 Statues white, and cool arcades,
Where at eve the German warrior
 Winks upon the German maids;—

Such is Munich:—broad and stately,
 Rich of hue, and fair of form;
But, towards the end of August,
 Unequivocally *warm.*

There, the long dim galleries threading,
 May the artist's eye behold
Breathing from the 'deathless canvas'
 Records of the years of old:

Pallas there, and Jove, and Juno,
  'Take' once more their 'walks abroad',
Under Titian's fiery woodlands
  And the saffron skies of Claude:

There the Amazons of Rubens
  Lift the failing arm to strike,
And the pale light falls in masses
  On the horsemen of Vandyke;

And in Berghem's pools reflected
  Hang the cattle's graceful shapes,
And Murillo's soft boy-faces
  Laugh amid the Seville grapes;

And all purest, loveliest fancies
  That in poets' souls may dwell
Started into shape and substance
  At the touch of Raphael. . . .

Thence we turned, what time the blackbird
  Pipes to vespers from his perch,
And from out the clattering city
  Pass'd into the silent church;

Mark'd the shower of sunlight breaking
  Thro' the crimson panes o'erhead,
And on pictured wall and window
  Read the histories of the dead:

Till the kneelers round us, rising,
  Crossed their foreheads and were gone;
And o'er aisle and arch and cornice,
  Layer on layer, the night came on.

12. TO THE EARL OF DORSET

Copenhagen, March 9, 1709

From frozen climes, and endless tracts of snow,
From streams which northern winds forbid to flow,
What present shall the muse to Dorset bring;
Or how, so near the pole, attempt to sing?
The hoary winter here conceals from sight
All pleasing objects which to verse invite.
The hills and dales, and the delightful woods,
The flow'ry plains, and silver-streaming floods,
By snow disguis'd, in bright confusion lie,
And with one dazzling waste fatigue the eye.
   No gentle breathing breeze prepares the spring,
No birds within the desert region sing.
The ships, unmov'd, the boist'rous winds defy,
While rattling chariots o'er the ocean fly.
The vast Leviathan wants room to play,
And spout his waters in the face of day.
The starving wolves along the main sea prowl,
And to the moon in icy valleys howl.
O'er many a shining league the level main
Here spreads itself into a glassy plain:
There solid billows of enormous size,
Alps of green ice, in wild disorder rise.
   And yet but lately have I seen, ev'n here,
The winter in a lovely dress appear.
Ere yet the clouds let fall the treasur'd snow,
Or winds begun through hazy skies to blow,
At ev'ning a keen eastern breeze arose,
And the descending rain unsully'd froze.
Soon as the silent shades of night withdrew,
The ruddy morn disclos'd at once to view
The face of nature in a rich disguise,
And brighten'd ev'ry object to my eyes:
For ev'ry shrub, and ev'ry blade of grass,
And ev'ry pointed thorn, seem'd wrought in glass;

In pearls and rubies rich the hawthorns show,
While through the ice the crimson berries glow.
The thick-sprung reeds, which watry marshes yield,
Seem'd polish'd lances in a hostile field.
The stag in limpid currents, with surprise,
Sees crystal branches on his forehead rise:
The spreading oak, the beech, and tow'ring pine,
Glaz'd over, in the freezing æther shine.
The frighted birds the rattling branches shun,
Which wave and glitter in the distant sun.
　　When if a sudden gust of wind arise,
The brittle forest into atoms flies,
The crackling wood beneath the tempest bends,
And in a spangled show'r the prospect ends:
Or, if a southern gale the region warm,
And by degrees unbind the wintry charm,
The traveller a miry country sees,
And journies sad beneath the dropping trees:
Like some deluded peasant, Merlin leads
Through fragrant bow'rs, and through delicious meads,
While here enchanted gardens to him rise,
And airy fabrics there attract his eyes,
His wand'ring feet the magick paths pursue,
And while he thinks the fair illusion true,
The trackless scenes disperse in fluid air,
And woods, and wilds, and thorny ways appear,
A tedious road the weary wretch returns,
And, as he goes, the transient vision mourns.

JAMES KENNETH STEPHEN 1859–1892

13. ENGLAND AND AMERICA

1. *On a Rhine Steamer*

Republic of the West,
　　Enlightened, free, sublime,
Unquestionably best
　　Production of our time.

17

The telephone is thine,
    And thine the Pullman Car,
The caucus, the divine
    Intense electric star.

To thee we likewise owe
    The venerable names
Of Edgar Allan Poe,
    And Mr. Henry James.

In short it's due to thee,
    Thou kind of Western star,
That we have come to be
    Precisely what we are.

But every now and then,
    It cannot be denied,
You breed a kind of men
    Who are not dignified,

Or courteous or refined,
    Benevolent or wise,
Or gifted with a mind
    Beyond the common size,

Or notable for tact,
    Agreeable to me,
Or anything, in fact
    That people ought to be.

2. *On a Parisian Boulevard*

Britannia rules the waves,
    As I have heard her say;
She frees whatever slaves
    She meets upon her way.

A teeming mother she
    Of Parliaments and Laws;
Majestic, mighty, free:
    Devoid of common flaws.

18

For her did Shakspere write
  His admirable plays:
For her did Nelson fight
  And Wolseley win his bays.

Her sturdy common sense
  Is based on solid grounds:
By saving numerous pence
  She spends effective pounds.

The Saxon and the Celt
  She equitably rules;
Her iron rod is felt
  By countless knaves and fools.

In fact, mankind at large,
  Black, yellow, white and red,
Is given to her in charge,
  And owns her as a head.

But every here and there—
  Deny it if you can—
She breeds a vacant stare
  Unworthy of a man:

A look of dull surprise;
  A nerveless idle hand:
An eye which never tries
  To threaten or command:

In short, a kind of man,
  If man indeed he be,
As worthy of our ban
  As any that we see:

Unspeakably obtuse,
  Abominably vain,
Of very little use,
  And execrably plain.

OLIVER GOLDSMITH 1728–1774

from
The Traveller

14. HOLLAND

To men of other minds my fancy flies,
Embosom'd in the deep where Holland lies.
Methinks her patient sons before me stand,
Where the broad ocean leans against the land,
And, sedulous to stop the coming tide,
Lift the tall rampire's artificial pride.
Onward methinks, and diligently slow,
The firm connected bulwark seems to grow;
Spreads its long arms amidst the watery roar,
Scoops out an empire, and usurps the shore.
While the pent ocean, rising o'er the pile,
Sees an amphibious world beneath him smile:
The slow canal, the yellow-blossom'd vale,
The willow-tufted bank, the gliding sail,
The crowded mart, the cultivated plain,—
A new creation rescued from his reign.

MATTHEW PRIOR 1664–1721

15. THE SECRETARY

Written at the Hague, in the year 1696

While with labour assid'ous due pleasure I mix,
And in one day atone for the bus'ness of six,
In a little Dutch-chaise on a Saturday night,
On my left hand my Horace, a Nymph on my right.
No memoire to compose, and no post-boy to move,
That on Sunday may hinder the softness of love;
For her, neither visits, nor parties of tea,
Nor the long-winded cant of a dull refugée.

20

This night and the next shall be hers, shall be mine,
To good or ill fortune the third we resign:
Thus scorning the world, and superior to fate,
I drive on my car in processional state;
So with Phia thro' Athens Pisistratus rode,
Men thought her Minerva, and him a new God.
But why should I stories of Athens rehearse,
Where people knew love, and were partial to verse,
Since none can with justice my pleasures oppose,
In Holland half drowned in int'rest and prose:
By Greece and past ages, what need I be tried,
When the Hague and the present, are both on my side,
And is it enough, for the joys of the day,
To think what Anacreon or Sappho would say.
When good Vandergoes and his provident Vrough,
As they gaze on my triumph, do freely allow,
That search all the province, you'd find no man *dar* is
So bless'd as the *Englishen Heer Secretar'* is.

DANTE GABRIEL ROSSETTI 1828–1882

16. THE STAIRCASE OF NOTRE DAME, PARIS

As one who, groping in a narrow stair,
    Hath a strong sound of bells upon his ears,
    Which, being at a distance off, appears
Quite close to him because of the pent air:
So with this France. She stumbles file and square
    Darkling and without space for breath: each one
    Who hears the thunder says: 'It shall anon
Be in among her ranks to scatter her'.

This may be; and it may be that the storm
    Is spent in rain upon the unscathed seas,
        Or wasteth other countries ere it die:
Till she,—having climbed always through the swarm
    Of darkness and of hurtling sound,—from these
        Shall step forth on the light in a still sky.

21

from
Aurora Leigh

17. FAIR FANTASTIC PARIS

. . . the terraced streets,
The glittering boulevards, the white colonnades
Of fair fantastic Paris who wears trees
Like plumes, as if man made them, spire and tower
As if they had grown by nature, tossing up
Her fountains in the sunshine of the squares,
As if in beauty's game she tossed the dice,
Or blew the silver down-balls of her dreams
To sow futurity with seeds of thought
And count the passage of her festive hours.

ROBERT BROWNING 1812–1889

18. WHAT'S BECOME OF WARING?

What's become of Waring
Since he gave us all the slip,
Chose land-travel or seafaring,
Boots and chest or staff and scrip,
Rather than pace up and down
Any longer London town? . . .

Ichabod, Ichabod,
The glory is departed!
Travels Waring East away?
Who, of knowledge, by hearsay,
Reports a man upstarted
Somewhere as a god,
Hordes grown European-hearted,
Millions of the wild made tame
On a sudden at his fame?
In Vishnu-land what Avatar?

Or who in Moscow, toward the Czar,
With the demurest of footfalls
Over the Kremlin's pavement bright
With serpentine and syenite,
Steps, with five other Generals
That simultaneously take snuff,
For each to have pretext enough
And kerchiefwise unfold his sash
Which, softness' self, is yet the stuff
To hold fast where a steel chain snaps,
And leave the grand white neck no gash?
Waring in Moscow, to those rough
Cold northern natures borne perhaps,
Like the lambwhite maiden dear
From the circle of mute kings
Unable to repress the tear,
Each as his sceptre down he flings,
To Dian's fane at Taurica,
Where now a captive priestess, she alway
Mingles her tender grave Hellenic speech
With theirs, tuned to the hailstone-beaten beach,
As pours some pigeon, from the myrrhy lands
Rapt by the whirlblast to fierce Scythian strands
Where breed the swallows, her melodious cry
Amid their barbarous twitter!
In Russia? Never! Spain were fitter!
Ay, most likely 'tis in Spain
That we and Waring meet again
Now, while he turns down that cool narrow lane
Into the blackness, out of grave Madrid
All fire and shine, abrupt as when there's slid
Its stiff gold blazing pall
From some black coffin-lid. . . .

from

The Spanish Gypsy

19. SPANISH SUNSET

The old rain-fretted mountains in their robes
Of shadow-broken gray; the rounded hills
Reddened with blood of Titans, whose huge limbs,
Entombed within, feed full the hardy flesh
Of cactus green and blue broad-sworded aloes;
The cypress soaring black above the lines
Of white court-walls; the jointed sugar-canes
Pale-golden with their feathers motionless
In the warm quiet:—all thought-teaching form
Utters itself in firm unshimmering hues.
For the great rock has screened the westering sun
That still on plains beyond streams vaporous gold
Among the branches; and within Bedmár
Has come the time of sweet serenity
When colour glows unglittering, and the soul
Of visible things shows silent happiness,
As that of lovers trusting though apart.

SIR THOMAS WYATT C. 1503–1542

20. OF HIS RETURN FROM SPAIN

Tagus, farewell, that westward with thy streams
Turns up the grains of gold already tried,
For I with spur and sail go seek the Thames,
Gainward the sun that sheweth her wealthy pride,
And to the town that Brutus sought by dreams,
Like bended moon that leans her lusty side.
My king, my country I seek, for whom I live;
O mighty Jove, the winds for this me give.

21. DON JUAN BIDS SPAIN A LONG FAREWELL

Don Juan stood, and, gazing from the stern,
   Beheld his native Spain receding far;
First partings form a lesson hard to learn,
   Even nations feel this when they go to war;
There is a sort of unexpressed concern,
   A kind of shock that sets one's heart ajar,
At leaving even the most unpleasant people
And places—one keeps looking at the steeple. . . .

'Farewell, my Spain! a long farewell!' he cried,
   'Perhaps I may revisit thee no more,
But die, as many an exiled heart hath died,
   Of its own thirst to see again thy shore:
Farewell, where Guadalquivir's waters glide!
   Farewell, my mother! and, since all is o'er,
Farewell, too, dearest Julia!—(here he drew
Her letter out again, and read it through.)

'And oh! if e'er I should forget, I swear—
   But that's impossible, and cannot be—
Sooner shall this blue Ocean melt to air,
   Sooner shall Earth resolve itself to sea,
Than I resign thine image, oh, my fair!
   Or think of anything, excepting thee;
A mind diseased no remedy can physic—
(Here the ship gave a lurch, and he grew seasick.)

'Sooner shall Heaven kiss earth—(here he fell sicker)
   Oh, Julia! what is every other woe?—
(For God's sake let me have a glass of liquor;
   Pedro, Battista, help me down below.)
Julia, my love!—(you rascal, Pedro, quicker)—
   Oh, Julia!—(this curst vessel pitches so)—
Belovèd Julia, hear me still beseeching!'
(Here he grew inarticulate with retching.)

He felt that chilling heaviness of heart,
  Or rather stomach, which, alas! attends,
Beyond the best apothecary's art,
  The loss of Love, the treachery of friends,
Or death of those we dote on, when a part
  Of us dies with them as each fond hope ends:
No doubt he would have been much more pathetic,
But the sea acted as a strong emetic. . . .

22. DON JUAN AND HIS TUTOR PEDRILLO ARE SHIPWRECKED

The ship, called the most holy 'Trinidada',
  Was steering duly for the port Leghorn;
For there the Spanish family Moncada
  Were settled long ere Juan's sire was born:
They were relations, and for them he had a
  Letter of introduction, which the morn
Of his departure had been sent him by
His Spanish friends for those in Italy.

His suite consisted of three servants and
  A tutor, the licentiate Pedrillo,
Who several languages did understand,
  But now lay sick and speechless on his pillow,
And, rocking in his hammock, longed for land,
  His headache being increased by every billow;
And the waves oozing through the port-hole made
His berth a little damp, and him afraid. . . .

'T was not without some reason, for the wind
  Increased at night, until it blew a gale;
And though 't was not much to a naval mind,
  Some landsmen would have looked a little pale,
For sailors are, in fact, a different kind:
  At sunset they began to take in sail,
For the sky showed it would come on to blow,
And carry away, perhaps, a mast or so.

At one o'clock the wind with sudden shift
    Threw the ship right into the trough of the sea,
Which struck her aft, and made an awkward rift,
    Started the stern-post, also shattered the
Whole of her stern-frame, and, ere she could lift
    Herself from out her present jeopardy,
The rudder tore away; 'twas time to sound
The pumps, and there were four feet water found.

One gang of people instantly was put
    Upon the pumps, and the remainder set
To get up part of the cargo, and what not;
    But they could not come at the leak as yet;
At last they did get at it really, but
    Still their salvation was an even bet:
The water rushed through in a way quite puzzling,
While they thrust sheets, shirts, jackets, bales of muslin,

Into the opening; but all such ingredients
    Would have been vain, and they must have gone down,
Despite of all their efforts and expedients,
    But for the pumps: I'm glad to make them known
To all the brother tars who may have need hence,
    For fifty tons of water were upthrown
By them per hour, and they had all been undone,
But for the maker, Mr. Mann, of London.

As day advanced the weather seemed to abate,
    And then the leak they reckoned to reduce,
And keep the ship afloat, though three feet yet
    Kept two hand- and one chain-pump still in use.
The wind blew fresh again: as it grew late
    A squall came on, and while some guns broke loose,
A gust—which all descriptive power transcends—
Laid with one blast the ship on her beam ends.

There she lay, motionless, and seemed upset;
    The water left the hold, and washed the decks,
And made a scene men do not soon forget;
    For they remember battles, fires, and wrecks,
Or any other thing that brings regret,
    Or breaks their hopes, or hearts, or heads, or necks:
Thus drownings are much talked of by the divers,
And swimmers, who may chance to be survivors.

Immediately the masts were cut away,
    Both main and mizen; first the mizen went,
The main-mast followed: but the ship still lay
    Like a mere log, and baffled our intent.
Foremast and bowsprit were cut down, and they
    Eased her at last (although we never meant
To part with all till every hope was blighted),
And then with violence the old ship righted. . . .

Under the vessel's keel the sail was passed,
    And for the moment it had some effect;
But with a leak, and not a stick of mast,
    Nor rag of canvas, what could they expect?
But still 'tis best to struggle to the last,
    'Tis never too late to be wholly wrecked:
And though 'tis true that man can only die once,
'Tis not so pleasant in the Gulf of Lyons. . . .

The worst of all was, that in their condition,
    Having been several days in great distress,
'Twas difficult to get out such provision
    As now might render their long suffering less:
Men, even when dying, dislike inanition;
    Their stock was damaged by the weather's stress:
Two casks of biscuit, and a keg of butter,
Were all that could be thrown into the cutter.

But in the long-boat they contrived to stow
    Some pounds of bread, though injured by the wet;
Water, a twenty-gallon cask or so;
    Six flasks of wine; and they contrived to get
A portion of their beef up from below,
    And with a piece of pork, moreover, met,
But scarce enough to serve them for a luncheon—
Then there was rum, eight gallons in a puncheon. . . .

'Twas twilight, and the sunless day went down
    Over the waste of waters; like a veil,
Which, if withdrawn, would but disclose the frown
    Of one whose hate is masked but to assail.
Thus to their hopeless eyes the night was shown,
    And grimly darkled o'er the faces pale,
And the dim desolate deep: twelve days had Fear
Been their familiar, and now Death was here.

Some trial had been making at a raft,
    With little hope in such a rolling sea,
A sort of thing at which one would have laughed,
    If any laughter at such times could be,
Unless with people who too much have quaffed,
    And have a kind of wild and horrid glee,
Half epileptical, and half hysterical:—
Their preservation would have been a miracle.

At half-past eight o'clock, booms, hencoops, spars,
    And all things, for a chance, had been cast loose,
That still could keep afloat the struggling tars,
    For yet they strove, although of no great use:
There was no light in heaven but a few stars,
    The boats put off o'ercrowded with their crews;
She gave a heel, and then a lurch to port,
And, going down head foremost—sunk, in short.

Then rose from sea to sky the wild farewell—
    Then shrieked the timid, and stood still the brave,—
Then some leaped overboard with dreadful yell,
    As eager to anticipate their grave;
And the sea yawned around her like a hell,
    And down she sucked with her the whirling wave,
Like one who grapples with his enemy,
And strives to strangle him before he die.

And first one universal shriek there rushed,
    Louder than the loud Ocean, like a crash
Of echoing thunder; and then all was hushed,
    Save the wild wind and the remorseless dash
Of billows; but at intervals there gushed,
    Accompanied by a convulsive splash,
A solitary shriek, the bubbling cry
Of some strong swimmer in his agony. . . .

A small old spaniel,—which had been Don José's,
    His father's, whom he loved, as ye may think,
For on such things the memory reposes
    With tenderness—stood howling on the brink,
Knowing, (dogs have such intellectual noses!)
    No doubt, the vessel was about to sink;
And Juan caught him up, and ere he stepped
Off threw him in, then after him he leaped. . . .

They counted thirty, crowded in a space
    Which left scarce room for motion or exertion;
They did their best to modify their case,
    One half sate up, though numbed with the immersion,
While t'other half were laid down in their place,
    At watch and watch; thus, shivering like the tertian
Ague in its cold fit, they filled their boat,
With nothing but the sky for a great coat. . . .

'Tis thus with people in an open boat,
    They live upon the love of Life, and bear
More than can be believed, or even thought,
    And stand like rocks the tempest's wear and tear;
And hardship still has been the sailor's lot,
    Since Noah's ark went cruising here and there;
She had a curious crew as well as cargo,
Like the first old Greek privateer, the Argo.

But man is a carnivorous production,
    And must have meals, at least one meal a day;
He cannot live, like woodcocks, upon suction,
    But, like the shark and tiger, must have prey;
Although his anatomical construction
    Bears vegetables, in a grumbling way,
Your labouring people think, beyond all question,
Beef, veal, and mutton, better for digestion. . . .

The fourth day came, but not a breath of air,
    And Ocean slumbered like an unweaned child:
The fifth day, and their boat lay floating there,
    The sea and sky were blue, and clear, and mild—
With their one oar (I wish they had had a pair)
    What could they do? and Hunger's rage grew wild:
So Juan's spaniel, spite of his entreating,
Was killed, and portioned out for present eating.

On the sixth day they fed upon his hide,
    And Juan, who had still refused, because
The creature was his father's dog that died,
    Now feeling all the vulture in his jaws,
With some remorse received (though first denied)
    As a great favour one of the fore-paws,
Which he divided with Pedrillo, who
Devoured it, longing for the other too.

The seventh day, and no wind—the burning sun
  Blistered and scorched, and, stagnant on the sea,
They lay like carcasses; and hope was none,
  Save in the breeze that came not: savagely
They glared upon each other—all was done,
  Water, and wine, and food,—and you might see
The longings of the cannibal arise
(Although they spoke not) in their wolfish eyes.

At length one whispered his companion, who
  Whispered another, and thus it went round,
And then into a hoarser murmur grew,
  An ominous, and wild, and desperate sound;
And when his comrade's thought each sufferer knew,
  'Twas but his own, suppressed till now, he found:
And out they spoke of lots for flesh and blood,
And who should die to be his fellow's food. . . .

The lots were made, and marked, and mixed, and handed,
  In silent horror, and their distribution
Lulled even the savage hunger which demanded
  Like the Promethean vulture, this pollution;
None in particular had sought or planned it,
  'Twas Nature gnawed them to this resolution,
By which none were permitted to be neuter—
And the lot fell on Juan's luckless tutor. . . .

The sailors ate him, all save three or four,
  Who were not quite so fond of animal food;
To these was added Juan, who, before
  Refusing his own spaniel, hardly could
Feel now his appetite increased much more;
  'Twas not to be expected that he should,
Even in extremity of their disaster,
Dine with them on his pastor and his master.

'Twas better that he did not; for, in fact,
  The consequence was awful in the extreme;
For they, who were most ravenous in the act,
  Went raging mad—Lord! how they did blaspheme!
And foam, and roll, with strange convulsions racked,
  Drinking salt-water like a mountain stream,
Tearing, and grinning, howling, screeching, swearing,
And, with hyæna laughter, died despairing. . . .

And the same night there fell a shower of rain,
  For which their mouths gaped, like the cracks of earth
When dried to summer dust; till taught by pain,
  Men really know not what good water's worth;
If you had been in Turkey or in Spain,
  Or with a famished boat's-crew had your berth,
Or in the desert heard the camel's bell,
You'd wish yourself where Truth is—in a well. . . .

And their baked lips, with many a bloody crack,
  Sucked in the moisture, which like nectar streamed;
Their throats were ovens, their swoln tongues were black,
  As the rich man's in Hell, who vainly screamed
To beg the beggar, who could not rain back
  A drop of dew, when every drop had seemed
To taste of Heaven—If this be true, indeed,
Some Christians have a comfortable creed. . . .

With twilight it again came on to blow,
  But not with violence; the stars shone out,
The boat made way; yet now they were so low,
  They knew not where or what they were about;
Some fancied they saw land, and some said 'No!'
  The frequent fog-banks gave them cause to doubt—
Some swore that they heard breakers, others guns,
And all mistook about the latter once

As morning broke, the light wind died away,
    When he who had the watch sung out and swore,
If 'twas not land that rose with the Sun's ray,
    He wished that land he never might see more;
And the rest rubbed their eyes and saw a bay,
    Or thought they saw, and shaped their course for shore;
For shore it was, and gradually grew
Distinct, and high, and palpable to view.

And then of these some part burst into tears,
    And others, looking with a stupid stare,
Could not yet separate their hopes from fears,
    And seemed as if they had no further care;
While a few prayed—(the first time for some years)—
    And at the bottom of the boat three were
Asleep: they shook them by the hand and head,
And tried to awaken them, but found them dead. . . .

The land appeared a high and rocky coast,
    And higher grew the mountains as they drew,
Set by a current, toward it: they were lost
    In various conjectures, for none knew
To what part of the earth they had been tost,
    So changeable had been the winds that blew;
Some thought it was Mount Ætna, some the highlands
Of Candia, Cyprus, Rhodes, or other islands. . . .

As they drew nigh the land, which now was seen
    Unequal in its aspect here and there,
They felt the freshness of its growing green,
    That waved in forest-tops, and smoothed the air,
And fell upon their glazed eyes like a screen
    From glistening waves, and skies so hot and bare—
Lovely seemed any object that should sweep
Away the vast—salt—dread—eternal Deep.

from
A Letter to Maria Gisborne. July 1, 1820

23. AT LEGHORN

I see a chaos of green leaves and fruit
Built round dark caverns, even to the root
Of the living stems that feed them—in whose bowers
There sleep in their dark dew the folded flowers;
Beyond, the surface of the unsickled corn
Trembles not in the slumbering air, and borne
In circles quaint, and ever-changing dance,
Like wingèd stars the fire-flies flash and glance,
Pale in the open moonshine, but each one
Under the dark trees seems a little sun,
A meteor tamed; a fixed star gone astray
From the silver regions of the milky way;—
Afar the Contadino's song is heard,
Rude, but made sweet by distance—and a bird
Which cannot be the Nightingale, and yet
I know none else that sings so sweet as it
At this late hour. . . .

WILLIAM WORDSWORTH 1770–1850

from
The Prelude, 1805

24. THAT PAIR OF GOLDEN DAYS

—Locarno, spreading out in width like Heaven,
And Como, thou, a treasure by the earth
Kept to itself, a darling bosom'd up
In Abyssinian privacy, I spake
Of thee, thy chestnut woods, and garden plots
Of Indian corn tended by dark-eyed Maids,
Thy lofty steeps, and pathways roof'd with vines
Winding from house to house, from town to town,

Sole link that binds them to each other, walks
League after league, and cloistral avenues
Where silence is, if music be not there:
While yet a Youth, undisciplin'd in Verse,
Through fond ambition of my heart, I told
Your praises; nor can I approach you now
Ungreeted by a more melodious Song,
Where tones of learned Art and Nature mix'd
May frame enduring language. Like a breeze
Or sunbeam over your domain I pass'd
In motion without pause; but Ye have left
Your beauty with me, an impassion'd sight
Of colours and of forms, whose power is sweet
And gracious, almost might I dare to say,
As virtue is, or goodness, sweet as love
Or the remembrance of a noble deed,
Or gentlest visitations of pure thought
When God, the Giver of all joy, is thank'd
Religiously, in silent blessedness,
Sweet as this last herself; for such it is.

Through those delightful pathways we advanc'd,
Two days, and still in presence of the Lake,
Which, winding up among the Alps, now chang'd
Slowly its lovely countenance, and put on
A sterner character. The second night,
In eagerness, and by report misled
Of those Italian clocks that speak the time
In fashion different from ours, we rose
By moonshine, doubting not that day was near,
And that, meanwhile, coasting the Water's edge
As hitherto, and with as plain a track
To be our guide, we might behold the scene
In its most deep repose.—We left the Town
Of Gravedona with this hope; but soon
Were lost, bewilder'd among woods immense,
Where, having wander'd for a while, we stopp'd
And on a rock sate down, to wait for day.
An open place it was, and overlook'd,
From high, the sullen water underneath,

On which a dull red image of the moon
Lay bedded, changing oftentimes its form
Like an uneasy snake: long time we sate,
For scarcely more than one hour of the night,
Such was our error, had been gone, when we
Renew'd our journey. On the rock we lay
And wish'd to sleep but could not, for the stings
Of insects, which with noise like that of noon
Fill'd all the woods; the cry of unknown birds,
The mountains, more by darkness visible
And their own size, than any outward light,
The breathless wilderness of clouds, the clock
That told with unintelligible voice
The widely-parted hours, the noise of streams
And sometimes rustling motions nigh at hand
Which did not leave us free from personal fear,
And lastly the withdrawing Moon, that set
Before us, while she still was high in heaven,
These were our food, and such a summer's night
Did to that pair of golden days succeed,
With now and then a doze and snatch of sleep,
On Como's Banks, the same delicious Lake.

JAMES THOMSON 1700–1748

25. VENICE FIXED IN THE SEAS BY THE GODDESS LIBERTY

The seeming god-built city! which my hand
Deep in the bosom fixed of wondering seas.
Astonished mortals sailed with pleasing awe
Around the sea-girt walls, by Neptune fenced,
And down the briny street, where on each hand,
Amazing seen amid unstable waves,
The splendid palace shines, and rising tides,
The green steps marking, murmur at the door.
To this fair queen of Adria's stormy gulf,
The mart of nations! long obedient seas
Rolled all the treasure of the radiant East.
But now no more. . . .

26. I RODE ONE EVENING WITH
COUNT MADDALO

I rode one evening with Count Maddalo
Upon the bank of land which breaks the flow
Of Adria towards Venice: a bare strand
Of hillocks, heaped from ever-shifting sand,
Matted with thistles and amphibious weeds,
Such as from earth's embrace the salt ooze breeds,
Is this; an uninhabited sea-side,
Which the lone fisher, when his nets are dried,
Abandons; and no other object breaks
The waste, but one dwarf tree and some few stakes
Broken and unrepaired, and the tide makes
A narrow space of level sand thereon,
Where 'twas our wont to ride while day went down. . . .

As those who pause on some delightful way
Tho' bent on pleasant pilgrimage, we stood
Looking upon the evening and the flood
Which lay between the city and the shore
Paved with the image of the sky . . . the hoar
And aëry Alps towards the North appeared
Thro' mist, an heaven-sustaining bulwark reared
Between the East and West; and half the sky
Was roofed with clouds of rich emblazonry
Dark purple at the zenith, which still grew
Down the steep West into a wondrous hue
Brighter than burning gold, even to the rent
Where the swift sun yet paused in his descent
Among the many folded hills: they were
Those famous Euganean hills, which bear,
As seen from Lido thro' the harbour piles,
The likeness of a clump of peakèd isles—
And then—as if the Earth and Sea had been
Dissolved into one lake of fire, were seen
Those mountains towering as from waves of flame

Around the vaporous sun, from which there came
The inmost purple spirit of light, and made
Their very peaks transparent. 'Ere it fade,'
Said my companion, 'I will show you soon
A better station'—so, o'er the lagune
We glided, and from that funereal bark
I leaned, and saw the city, and could mark
How from their many isles in evening's gleam
Its temples and its palaces did seem
Like fabrics of enchantment piled to Heaven.

THOMAS MOORE 1779–1852

from

Rhymes on the Road

27. VENICE

And is there then no earthly place,
   Where we can rest, in dream Elysian,
Without some curst, round English face,
   Popping up near, to break the vision?
'Mid northern lakes, mid southern vines,
   Unholy cits we're doom'd to meet;
Nor highest Alps nor Appenines
   Are sacred from Threadneedle Street!

If up the Simplon's path we wind,
Fancying we leave this world behind,
Such pleasant sounds salute one's ear
As—'Baddish news from 'Change, my dear—
The Funds—(phew, curse this ugly hill)—
Are low'ring fast—(what, higher still?)—
And—(zooks, we're mounting up to heaven!)—
Will soon be down to sixty-seven.'

Go where we may—rest where we will,
Eternal London haunts us still.
The trash of Almack's or Fleet Ditch—
And scarce a pin's head difference *which*—

Mixes, though ev'n to Greece we run,
With every rill from Helicon!
And, if this rage for travelling lasts,
If Cockneys, of all sects and castes,
Old maidens, aldermen, and squires,
Will leave their puddings and coal fires,
To gape at things in foreign lands,
No soul among them understands;
If Blues desert their coteries,
To show off 'mong the Wahabees;
If neither sex nor age controls,
   Nor fear of Mamelukes forbids
Young ladies, with pink parasols,
   To glide among the Pyramids—
Why, then, farewell all hope to find
A spot, that's free from London-kind!
Who knows, if to the West we roam,
But we may find some *Blue* 'at home'
   Among the *Blacks* of Carolina—
Or, flying to the Eastward, see
Some Mrs. Hopkins, taking tea
   And toast upon the Wall of China!

DAVID HERBERT LAWRENCE 1885–1930

28. BAT

At evening, sitting on this terrace,
When the sun from the west, beyond Pisa, beyond the mountains of
   Carrara
Departs, and the world is taken by surprise . . .

When the tired flower of Florence is in gloom beneath the glowing
Brown hills surrounding . . .

When under the arches of the Ponte Vecchio
A green light enters against stream, flush from the west,
Against the current of obscure Arno . . .

40

Look up, and you see things flying
Between the day and the night;
Swallows with spools of dark thread sewing the shadows together.

A circle swoop, and a quick parabola under the bridge arches
Where light pushes through;
A sudden turning upon itself of a thing in the air.
A dip to the water.

And you think:
'The swallows are flying so late!'

Swallows?

Dark air-life looping
Yet missing the pure loop . . .
A twitch, a twitter, an elastic shudder in flight
And serrated wings against the sky,
Like a glove, a black glove thrown up at the light,
And falling back.

Never swallows!
Bats!
The swallows are gone.

At a wavering instant the swallows give way to bats
By the Ponte Vecchio . . .
Changing guard.

Bats, and an uneasy creeping in one's scalp
As the bats swoop overhead!
Flying madly.

Pipistrello!
Black piper on an infinitesimal pipe.
Little lumps that fly in air and have voices indefinite, wildly
    vindictive;

Wings like bits of umbrella.

Bats!

Creatures that hang themselves up like an old rag, to sleep;
And disgustingly upside down.

Hanging upside down like rows of disgusting old rags
And grinning in their sleep.
Bats!

In China the bat is symbol of happiness.

Not for me!

WILLIAM SHAKESPEARE 1564–1616

from
Twelfth Night

29. MEMORIALS AND THE THINGS OF FAME

Sebastian: What's to do?
    Shall we go see the reliques of this town?

Antonio:
    To-morrow, sir: best first go see your lodging.

Sebastian:
        I am not weary, and 'tis long to night:
        I pray you, let us satisfy our eyes
        With the memorials and the things of fame
        That do renown this city.

from
Paradise Regain'd

30. ROME

The City which thou seest no other deem
Then great and glorious *Rome*, Queen of the Earth
So far renown'd, and with the spoils enricht
Of Nations; there the Capitol thou seest
Above the rest lifting his stately head
On the *Tarpeian* rock, her Cittadel
Impregnable, and there Mount *Palatine*
The Imperial Palace, compass huge, and high
The Structure, skill of noblest Architects,
With gilded battlements, conspicuous far,
Turrets and Terrases, and glittering Spires.
Many a fair Edifice besides, more like
Houses of Gods (so well I have dispos'd
My Aerie Microscope) thou may'st behold
Outside and inside both, pillars and roofs
Carv'd work, the hand of fam'd Artificers
In Cedar, Marble, Ivory or Gold.
Thence to the gates cast round thine eye, and see
What conflux issuing forth, or entring in, . . .
Pretors, Proconsuls to their Provinces
Hasting or on return, in robes of State;
Lictors and rods the ensigns of thir power,
Legions and Cohorts, turmes of horse and wings:
Or Embassies from Regions far remote
In various habits on the *Appian* road,
Or on the *Æmilian*, some from farthest South,
Syene, and where the shadow both way falls,
Meroe, *Nilotic* Isle, and more to West,
The Realm of *Bocchus* to the Black-moor Sea;
From the *Asian* Kings and *Parthian* among these,
From *India* and the golden *Chersoness*,
And utmost *Indian* Isle *Taprobane*,
Dusk faces with white silken Turbants wreath'd.

31. AT ROME

O richly soiled and richly sunned,
Exuberant, fervid, and fecund!
  Is this the fixed condition
On which may Northern pilgrim come,
To imbibe thine ether-air, and sum
  Thy store of old tradition?
Must we be chill, if clean, and stand
Foot-deep in dirt on classic land?

So is it: in all ages so,
And in all places man can know,
From homely roots unseen below,
The stem in forest, field and bower,
Derives the emanative power
That crowns it with the ethereal flower,
From mixtures fœtid, foul, and sour
Draws juices that those petals fill.

Ah Nature, if indeed thy will
Thou own'st it, it shall not be ill!
And truly here, in this quick clime,
Where, scarcely bound by space or time,
The elements in half a day
Toss off with exquisitest play
What our cold seasons toil and grieve,
And never quite at last achieve;
Where processes, with pain, and fear,
Disgust, and horror wrought, appear
The quick mutations of a dance,
Wherein retiring but to advance,
Life, in brief interpause of death,
One moment sitting taking breath,
Forth comes again as glad as e'er,
In some new figure full as fair,
Where what has scarcely ceased to be,
Instinct with newer birth we see—
What dies, already, look you, lives;
In such a clime, who thinks, forgives;

44

Who sees, will understand; who knows,
In calm of knowledge find repose,
And thoughtful as of glory gone,
So too of more to come anon,
Of permanent existence sure,
Brief intermediate breaks endure.
  O Nature, if indeed thy will,
Thou ownest it, it is not ill!
And e'en as oft on heathy hill,
On moorland black, and ferny fells,
Beside thy brooks and in thy dells,
Was welcomed erst the kindly stain
Of thy true earth, e'en so again
With resignation fair, and meet
The dirt and refuse of thy street,
My philosophic foot shall greet,
So leave but perfect to my eye
Thy columns, set against thy sky!

JOHN HENRY NEWMAN 1801–1890

32. THE GOOD SAMARITAN

Palermo, June 13, 1833

Oh that thy creed were sound!
For thou dost soothe the heart, thou Church of Rome,
  By thy unwearied watch and varied round
Of service, in thy Saviour's holy home.
  I cannot walk the city's sultry streets,
  But the wide porch invites to still retreats,
Where passion's thirst is calm'd, and care's unthankful
    gloom.

    There, on a foreign shore,
The homesick solitary finds a friend:
  Thoughts, prison'd long for lack of speech, outpour
Their tears; and doubts in resignation end.
  I almost fainted from the long delay
  That tangles me within this languid bay,
When comes a foe, my wounds with oil and wine to tend.

45

33. LETTER FROM SMYRNA
TO HIS SISTERS AT CRUX-EASTON, 1733

The hero who to Smyrna bay
From Easton, Hants, pursu'd his way,
Who travers'd seas, and hills and vales,
To fright his sisters with his tales,
Sing heavenly Muse; for what befel
Thou saw'st, and only thou can'st tell . . .
Say first, those very rocks we spy'd,
But left 'em on the starboard side,
Where Juno urg'd the Trojan's fate.
Shield us, ye Gods, from female hate! . . .
What saw we on Sicilian ground?
(A soil in ancient verse renown'd)
The self-same spot, or Virgil ly'd,
On which the good Anchises dy'd;
The field where Ceres' daughter sported,
And where the pretty Cyclops courted.
The nymph hard-hearted as the rocks,
Refus'd the monster, scorn'd his flocks,
And took a shepherd in his stead,
With nought but love and worth to plead:
An instance of a generous mind
That does much honour to your kind,
But in an age of fables grew,
So possibly it mayn't be true.
While on the summit Ætna glows,
His shivering sides are chill'd with snows.
Beneath, the painted landskip charms;
Here infant Spring in Winter's arms
Wantons secure; in youthful pride
Stands Summer laughing by her side;
Ev'n Autumn's yellow robes appear,
And one gay scene discloses all the year.
    Hence to rude Cerigo we came,
Known once by Cytherea's name;

When Ocean first the goddess bore,
She rose on this distinguish'd shore.
Here first the happy Paris stopp'd,
When Helen from her lord elop'd.
With pleas'd reflection I survey'd
Each secret grott, each conscious shade;
Envy'd his choice, approv'd his flame,
And fondly wish'd my lot the same. . . .

   How did my heart with joy run o'er,
When to the fam'd Cecropian shore,
Wafted by gentle breezes, we
Came gliding thro' the smooth still sea!
While backward rov'd my busy thought
On deeds in distant ages wrought;
On tyrants gloriously withstood;
On seas distain'd with Persian blood;
On trophies rais'd o'er hills of slain
In Marathon's unrival'd plain.
Then, as around I cast my eye,
And view'd the pleasing prospect nigh,
The land for arms and arts renown'd,
Where wit was honour'd, poets crown'd;
Whose manners and whose rules refin'd
Our souls, and civiliz'd mankind;
Or (yet a loftier pitch to raise
Our wonder, and compleat its praise)
The land that Plato's master bore—
How did my heart with joy run o'er!

   Now coasting on the eastern side,
We peep'd where Peneus rolls his tide:
Where Arethusa came t'appease
The shepherd that had lost his bees,
And led him to Cyrene's grott;
'Tis a long tale, and matters not.
Dryden will tell you all that past;
See, Virgil's Georgics, book the last.
I speak on't, but to let you know
This grott still stands in statu quo;
Of which if any doubts remain,
I've proof, as follows, clear and plain.

Here, sisters, we such honours met!
Such honours I shall ne'er forget.
The Goddess (no uncommon case)
Proud, I suppose, to shew her place,
Or piqu'd perhaps at your renown,
Sent Boreas to invite us down;
And he so press'd it, that we us'd
Some pains to get ourselves excus'd.
My brother shipmates, all in haste
Declar'd, that shells were not their taste;
And I had somewhere seen, you know,
A finer grott than she could shew.

Hence let the Muse to Delos roam,
Or Nio, fam'd for Homer's tomb;
To Naxos, known in ancient time,
For Bacchus' love, for Theseus' crime.
Can she the Lesbian vine forget
Whence Horace reinforc'd his wit?
Where the fam'd harp Arion strung
Nor play'd more sweet than Sappho sung?
Could the old bards revive again,
How would they mourn th' inverted scene!
Scarce with the barren waste acquainted,
They once so beautifully painted.

And here, 'twixt friends, I needs must say,
But let it go no farther, pray,
These sung-up, cry'd up countries are
Displeasing, rugged, black, and bare;
And all I've yet beheld or known
Serve only to endear my own.

The matters I shall next disclose,
'Tis likely may be wrapp'd in prose;
But verse methought would suit these better,
Besides, it lengthens out my letter.
Read them, dear girls, with kind regard,
What comes so far, what comes so hard;
And to our mother too make known,
How travelling has improv'd her son.

Let not malicious critics join
Pope's homespun rhimes in rank with mine,

Form'd on that very spot of earth,
Where Homer's self receiv'd his birth;
Add, as I said, t'enhance their worth,
The pains they cost in bringing forth;
While his, as all mankind agrees,
Tho' wrote with care, are wrote with ease.

ANNE FINCH, COUNTESS OF WINCHILSEA 1661–1720

34. TO A FRIEND IN PRAISE OF THE INVENTION OF WRITING LETTERS

Blest be the man! his memory at least,
Who found the art, thus to unfold his breast,
And taught succeeding times an easy way
Their secret thoughts by letters to convey;
To baffle absence, and secure delight,
Which, till that time, was limited to sight.
The parting farewell spoke, the last adieu,
The less'ning distance past, then loss of view,
The friend was gone, which some kind moments gave,
And absence separated, like the grave.
The wings of Love were tender too, till then
No quill, thence pull'd, was shap'd into a pen,

To send in paper-sheets, from town to town,
Words smooth as they, and softer than his down.
O'er such he reign'd, whom neighbourhood had join'd,
And hopt, from bough to bough, supported by the wind.
When for a wife the youthful Patriarch sent,
The camels, jewels, and the steward went,
A wealthy equipage, tho' grave and slow;
But not a line, that might the lover shew.
The rings and bracelets woo'd her hands and arms;
But had she known of melting words, the charms
That under secret seals in ambush lie,
To catch the soul, when drawn into the eye,
The fair Assyrian had not took this guide,
Nor her soft heart in chains of pearl been ty'd.

49

Had these conveyances been then in date,
Joseph had known his wretched father's state,
Before a famine, which his life pursues,
Had sent his other sons, to tell the news.

Oh! might I live to see an art arise,
As this to thoughts, indulgent to the eyes;
That the dark pow'rs of distance could subdue,
And make me *see*, as well as *talk* to you;
That tedious miles, nor tracts of air might prove
Bars to my sight, and shadows to my love!
Yet were it granted, such unbounded things
Are wand'ring wishes, born on fancy's wings,
They'd stretch themselves beyond this happy case,
And ask an art, to help us to embrace.

HERMAN MELVILLE 1819–1891

35. THE ATTIC LANDSCAPE

Tourist, spare the avid glance
    That greedy roves the sight to see:
Little here of 'Old Romance',
    Or Picturesque of Tivoli.

No flushful tint the sense to warm—
Pure outline pale, a linear charm.
The clear-cut hills carved temples face,
Respond, and share their sculptural grace.

'Tis Art and Nature lodged together,
    Sister by sister, cheek to cheek;
Such Art, such Nature and such weather,
    The All-in-All seems here a Greek.

from

Paradise Regain'd

36. ATHENS

         . . . behold
Where on the *Ægean* shore a City stands
Built nobly, pure the air, and light the soil,
Athens the eye of *Greece*, Mother of Arts
And Eloquence, native to famous wits
Or hospitable, in her sweet recess,
City or Suburban, studious walks and shades;
See there the Olive Grove of *Academe*,
Plato's retirement, where the *Attic* Bird
Trills her thick-warbl'd notes the summer long,
There flowrie hill *Hymettus* with the sound
Of Bees industrious murmur oft invites
To studious musing; there *Ilissus* rouls
His whispering stream. . . .

THOMAS GRAY 1716–1771

from

The Progress of Poesy

37. FORSAKEN PARNASSUS

  Woods, that wave o'er Delphi's steep,
Isles, that crown th' Egæan deep,
Fields, that cool Ilissus laves,
Or where Mæander's amber waves
In lingering Lab'rinths creep,
How do your tuneful Echos languish,
Mute, but to the voice of Anguish?
Where each old poetic Mountain
Inspiration breath'd around:

Ev'ry shade and hallow'd Fountain
Murmur'd deep a solemn sound:
Till the sad Nine in Greece's evil hour
Left their Parnassus for the Latian plains.
Alike they scorn the pomp of tyrant-Power,
And coward Vice, that revels in her chains.
When Latium had her lofty spirit lost,
They sought, oh Albion! next thy sea-encircled coast.

LAWRENCE DURRELL b. 1911

38. NEMEA

A song in the valley of Nemea:
Sing quiet, quite quiet here.

Song for the brides of Argos
Combing the swarms of golden hair:
Quite quiet, quiet there.

Under the rolling comb of grass,
The sword outrusts the golden helm.

Agamemnon under tumulus serene
Outsmiles the jury of skeletons:
Cool under cumulus the lion queen:

Only the drum can celebrate,
Only the adjective outlive them.

A song in the valley of Nemea:
Sing quiet, quiet, quiet here.

Tone of the frog in the empty well,
Drone of the bald bee on the cold skull,

Quiet, Quiet, Quiet.

39. HEATHEN GREECE

A Song

Where are the Islands of the Blest?
    They stud the Aegean Sea;
And where the deep Elysian rest?
    It haunts the vale where Peneus strong
    Pours his incessant stream along,
    While craggy ridge and mountain bare
    Cut keenly through the liquid air,
    And, in their own pure tints array'd,
    Scorn earth's green robes which change and fade,
    And stand in beauty undecay'd,
      Guards of the bold and free.

For what is Afric, but the home
    Of burning Phlegethon?
What the low beach and silent gloom,
    And chilling mists of that dull river,
    Along whose bank the thin ghosts shiver,—
    The thin wan ghosts that once were men,—
    But Tauris, isle of moor and fen,
    Or, dimly traced by seamen's ken,
      The pale-cliff'd Albion.

from
The Strayed Reveller

40. THE PORTICO OF CIRCE'S PALACE. EVENING

A Youth.   Circe.   Ulysses.

The Youth:

The Gods are happy.
They turn on all sides
Their shining eyes:
And see, below them,
The earth, and men.

They see Tiresias
Sitting, staff in hand,
On the warm, grassy
Asopus' bank:
His robe drawn over
His old, sightless head:
Revolving inly
The doom of Thebes.

They see the Centaurs
In the upper glens
Of Pelion, in the streams,
Where red-berried ashes fringe
The clear-brown shallow pools;
With streaming flanks, and heads
Rear'd proudly, snuffing
The mountain wind.

They see the Indian
Drifting, knife in hand,
His frail boat moor'd to
A floating isle thick matted
With large-leav'd, low creeping melon-plants,
And the dark cucumber.
He reaps, and stows them,

Drifting—drifting:—round him,
Round his green harvest-plot,
Flow the cool lake-waves:
The mountains ring them.

They see the Scythian
On the wide Stepp, unharnessing
His wheel'd house at noon.
He tethers his beast down, and makes his meal,
Mares' milk and bread
Bak'd on the embers:—all around
The boundless, waving grass-plains stretch, thick-starr'd
With saffron and the yellow hollyhock
And flag-leav'd iris flowers.
Sitting in his cart
He makes his meal: before him, for long miles,
Alive with bright green lizards,
And the springing bustard fowl,
The track, a straight black line,
Furrows the rich soil: here and there
Clusters of lonely mounds
Topp'd with rough-hewn
Grey, rain-blear'd statues, overpeer
The sunny Waste.

They see the Ferry
On the broad, clay-laden
Lone Chorasmian stream: thereon
With snort and strain,
Two horses, strongly swimming, tow
The ferry-boat, with woven ropes
To either bow
Firm harness'd by the mane:—a chief,
With shout and shaken spear
Stands at the prow, and guides them; but astern,
The cowering Merchants, in long robes,
Sit pale beside their wealth
Of silk bales and of balsam-drops,
Of gold and ivory,

Of turquoise-earth and amethyst,
Jasper and chalcedony,
And milk-barr'd onyx-stones.
The loaded boat swings groaning
In the yellow eddies.
The Gods behold them.

They see the Heroes
Sitting in the dark ship
On the foamless, long-heaving,
Violet sea:
At sunset nearing
The Happy Islands.

These things, Ulysses,
The wise Bards also
Behold and sing.
But oh, what labour!
O Prince, what pain!

LADY MARY WORTLEY MONTAGU 1689–1762

41. VERSES WRITTEN IN THE CHIOSK AT PERA, OVERLOOKING CONSTANTINOPLE

December 26, 1718

Give me, great God! said I, a little farm,
In summer shady, and in winter warm;
Where a clear spring gives birth to murm'ring brooks,
By nature gliding down the mossy rocks.
Not artfully by leaden pipes convey'd,
Or greatly falling in a forc'd cascade,
Pure and unsullied winding thro' the shade.
All bounteous Heaven has added to my prayer,
A softer climate and a purer air.

Our frozen isle now chilling winter binds,
Deform'd by rains, and rough with blasting winds;
The wither'd woods grow white with hoary frost,
By driving storms their verdant beauty lost;
The trembling birds their leafless covert shun,
And seek in distant climes a warmer sun:
The water-nymphs their silent urns deplore,
Ev'n Thames, benumb'd, 's a river now no more:
The barren meads no longer yield delight,
By glist'ning snows made painful to the sight.

Here summer reigns with one eternal smile,
Succeeding harvests bless the happy soil;
Fair fertile fields, to whom indulgent Heaven
Has ev'ry charm of ev'ry season given.
No killing cold deforms the beauteous year,
The springing flowers no coming winter fear.
But as the parent rose decays and dies,
The infant buds with brighter colour rise,
And with fresh sweets the mother's scent supplies.

Near them the violet grows with odours blest,
And blooms in more than Tyrian purple drest;
The rich jonquils their golden beams display,
And shine in glory's emulating day;
The peaceful groves their verdant leaves retain,
The streams still murmur undefil'd with rain,
And tow'ring greens adorn the fruitful plain.
The warbling kind uninterrupted sing,
Warmed with enjoyments of perpetual spring.

Here, at my window, I at once survey
The crowded city and resounding sea;
In distant views the Asian mountains rise,
And lose their snowy summits in the skies;
Above these mountains proud Olympus tow'rs,
The parliamental seat of heavenly pow'rs.
New to the sight my ravish'd eyes admire
Each gilded crescent and each antique spire,
The marble mosques, beneath whose ample domes
Fierce warlike sultans sleep in peaceful tombs;
Those lofty structures, once the Christian's boast,
Their names, their beauty, and their honours lost;

Those altars bright with gold and sculpture grac'd,
By barb'rous zeal of savage foes defac'd;
Soph'a alone, her ancient name retains,
Tho' th' unbeliever now her shrine profanes;
Where holy saints have died in sacred cells,
Where monarchs pray'd, the frantic dervise dwells.
How art thou fall'n, imperial city, low!
Where are thy hopes of Roman glory now?
Where are thy palaces by prelates rais'd?
Where Grecian artists all their skill display'd,
Before the happy sciences decay'd;
So vast, that youthful kings might here reside,
So splendid, to content a patriarch's pride;
Convents where emperors profess'd of old,
The labour'd pillars that their triumphs told;
Vain monuments of them that once were great,
Sunk undistinguish'd by one common fate;
One little spot the tenure small contains,
Of Greek nobility the poor remains;
Where other Helens, with like powerful charms,
Had once engag'd the warring world in arms;
Those names which royal ancestors can boast,
In mean mechanic arts obscurely lost;
Those eyes a second Homer might inspire,
Fix'd at the loom, destroy their useless fire:
Griev'd at a view, which struck upon my mind
The short-liv'd vanity of humankind.

In gaudy objects I indulge my sight,
And turn where Eastern pomp gives gay delight;
See the vast train in various habits drest,
By the bright scimitar and sable vest
The proud vizier distinguish'd o'er the rest!
Six slaves in gay attire his bridle hold,
His bridle rich with gems, and stirrups gold:
His snowy steed adorn'd with costly pride,
Whole troops of soldiers mounted by his side,
These top the plumy crest Arabian courtiers guide.
With artful duty all decline their eyes,
No bellowing shouts of noisy crowds arise;
Silence, in solemn state, the march attends,

Till at the dread divan the slow procession ends.
   Yet not these prospects all profusely gay,
The gilded navy that adorns the sea,
The rising city in confusion fair,
Magnificently form'd, irregular,
Where woods and palaces at once surprise,
Gardens on gardens, domes on domes arise,
And endless beauties tire the wand'ring eyes,
So soothe my wishes, or so charm my mind,
As this retreat secure from humankind.
No knave's successful craft does spleen excite,
No coxcomb's tawdry splendour shocks my sight,
No mob-alarm awakes my female fear,
No praise my mind, nor envy hurts my ear,
Ev'n fame itself can hardly reach me here;
Impertinence, with all her tattling train,   .
Fair-sounding flattery's delicious bane;
Censorious folly, noisy party rage,
The thousand tongues with which she must engage
Who dares have virtue in a vicious age.

WILLIAM BUTLER YEATS 1865–1939

(i)

42. SAILING TO BYZANTIUM

That is no country for old men. The young
In one another's arms, birds in the trees,
—Those dying generations—at their song,
The salmon-falls, the mackerel-crowded seas,
Fish, flesh, or fowl, commend all summer long
Whatever is begotten, born, and dies.
Caught in that sensual music all neglect
Monuments of unageing intellect.

59

An aged man is but a paltry thing,
A tattered coat upon a stick, unless
Soul clap its hands and sing, and louder sing
For every tatter in its mortal dress,
Nor is there singing school but studying
Monuments of its own magnificence;
And therefore I have sailed the seas and come
To the holy city of Byzantium.

O sages standing in God's holy fire
As in the gold mosaic of a wall,
Come from the holy fire, perne in a gyre,
And be the singing-masters of my soul.
Consume my heart away; sick with desire
And fastened to a dying animal
It knows not what it is; and gather me
Into the artifice of eternity.

Once out of nature I shall never take
My bodily form from any natural thing,
But such a form as Grecian goldsmiths make
Of hammered gold and gold enamelling
To keep a drowsy Emperor awake;
Or set upon a golden bough to sing
To lords and ladies of Byzantium
Of what is past, or passing, or to come.

(ii)

43. BYZANTIUM

The unpurged images of day recede;
The Emperor's drunken soldiery are abed;
Night resonance recedes, night-walkers' song
After great cathedral gong;
A starlit or a moonlit dome disdains
All that man is,
All mere complexities,
The fury and the mire of human veins.

Before me floats an image, man or shade,
Shade more than man, more image than a shade;
For Hades' bobbin bound in mummy-cloth
May unwind the winding path;
A mouth that has no moisture and no breath
Breathless mouths may summon;
I hail the superhuman;
I call it death-in-life and life-in-death.

Miracle, bird or golden handiwork,
More miracle than bird or handiwork,
Planted on the star-lit golden bough,
Can like the cocks of Hades crow,
Or, by the moon embittered, scorn aloud
In glory of changeless metal
Common bird or petal
And all complexities of mire or blood.

At midnight on the Emperor's pavement flit
Flames that no faggot feeds, nor steel has lit,
Nor storm disturbs, flames begotten of flame,
Where blood-begotten spirits come
And all complexities of fury leave,
Dying into a dance,
An agony of trance,
An agony of flame that cannot singe a sleeve.

Astraddle on the dolphin's mire and blood,
Spirit after spirit! The smithies break the flood,
The golden smithies of the Emperor!
Marbles of the dancing floor
Break bitter furies of complexity,
Those images that yet
Fresh images beget,
That dolphin-torn, that gong-tormented sea.

44. JOURNEY OF THE MAGI

'A cold coming we had of it,
Just the worst time of the year
For a journey, and such a long journey:
The ways deep and the weather sharp,
The very dead of winter.'
And the camels galled, sore-footed, refractory,
Lying down in the melting snow.
There were times we regretted
The summer palaces on slopes, the terraces,
And the silken girls bringing sherbet.
Then the camel men cursing and grumbling
And running away, and wanting their liquor and women,
And the night-fires going out, and the lack of shelters,
And the cities hostile and the towns unfriendly
And the villages dirty and charging high prices:
A hard time we had of it.
At the end we preferred to travel all night,
Sleeping in snatches,
With the voices singing in our ears, saying
That this was all folly.

Then at dawn we came down to a temperate valley,
Wet, below the snow line, smelling of vegetation;
With a running stream and a water-mill beating the darkness,
And three trees on the low sky,
And an old white horse galloped away in the meadow.
Then we came to a tavern with vine-leaves over the lintel,
Six hands at an open door dicing for pieces of silver,
And feet kicking the empty wine-skins.
But there was no information, and so we continued
And arrived at evening, not a moment too soon
Finding the place; it was (you may say) satisfactory.

All this was a long time ago, I remember,
And I would do it again, but set down
This set down
This: were we led all that way for

Birth or Death? There was a Birth, certainly,
We had evidence and no doubt. I had seen birth and death,
But had thought they were different; this Birth was
Hard and bitter agony for us, like Death, our death.
We returned to our places, these Kingdoms,
But no longer at ease here, in the old dispensation,
With an alien people clutching their gods.
I should be glad of another death.

EDMUND SPENSER C. 1552–1599

from

The Faerie Queene

45. UNA AND THE RED CROSS KNIGHT BEHOLD THE NEW JERUSALEM

[*Contemplation is to be their guide*]

Who when these two approching he aspide,
    At their first presence grew agrieued sore,
    That forst him lay his heauenly thoughts aside;
    And had he not that Dame respected more,
    Whom highly he did reuerence and adore,
    He would not once haue moued for the knight.
    They him saluted standing far afore;
    Who well them greeting, humbly did requight,
And asked, to what end they clomb that tedious height.

What end (quoth she) should cause vs take such paine,
    But that same end, which euery liuing wight
    Should make his marke, high heauen to attaine?
    Is not from hence the way, that leadeth right
    To that most glorious house, that glistreth bright
    With burning starres, and euerliuing fire,
    Whereof the keyes are to thy hand behight
    By wise *Fidelia?* she doth thee require,
To shew it to this knight, according his desire.

63

Thrise happy man, said then the father graue,
  Whose staggering steps thy steady hand doth lead,
  And shewes the way, his sinfull soule to saue.
  Who better can the way to heauen aread,
  Then thou thy selfe, that was both borne and bred
  In heauenly throne, where thousand Angels shine?
  Thou doest the prayers of the righteous sead
  Present before the majestie diuine,
And his auenging wrath to clemencie incline.

Yet since thou bidst, thy pleasure shalbe donne.
  Then come thou man of earth, and see the way,
  That neuer yet was seene of Faeries sonne,
  That neuer leads the traueiler astray,
  But after labours long, and sad delay,
  Brings them to ioyous rest and endlesse blis.
  But first thou must a season fast and pray,
  Till from her bands the spright assoiled is,
And haue her strength recur'd from fraile infirmitis.

That done, he leads him to the highest Mount;
  Such one, as that same mighty man of God,
  That bloud-red billowes like a walled front
  On either side disparted with his rod,
  Till that his army dry-foot through them yod,
  Dwelt fortie dayes vpon; where writ in stone
  With bloudy letters by the hand of God,
  The bitter doome of death and baleful mone
He did receiue, whiles flashing fire about him shone.

Or like that sacred hill, whose head full hie,
  Adornd with fruitful Oliues all arownd,
  Is, as it were for endlesse memory
  Of that deare Lord, who oft thereon was fownd,
  For euer with a flowring girlond crownd:
  Or like that pleasaunt Mount, that is for ay
  Through famous Poets verse each where renownd,
  On which the thrise three learned Ladies play
Their heauenly notes, and make full many a louely lay.

From thence, far off he vnto him did shew
    A litle path, that was both steepe and long,
    Which to a goodly Citie led his vew;
    Whose wals and towres were builded high and strong
    Of perle and precious stone, that earthly tong
    Cannot describe, nor wit of man can tell;
    Too high a ditty for my simple song;
    The Citie of the great king hight it well,
Wherein eternall peace and happinesse doth dwell.

As he thereon stood gazing, he might see
    The blessed Angels to and fro descend
    From highest heauen, in gladsome companee,
    And with great joy into that Citie wend,
    As commonly as friend does with his frend.
    Whereat he wondred much, and gan enquere,
    What stately building durst so high extend
    Her loftie towres vnto the starry sphere,
And what vnknowen nation there empeopled were.

Faire knight (quoth he) *Hierusalem* that is,
    The new *Hierusalem*, that God has built
    For those to dwell in, that are chosen his,
    His chosen people purg'd from sinfull guilt,
    With pretious bloud, which cruelly was spilt
    On cursed tree, of that vnspotted lam,
    That for the sinnes of all the world was kilt:
    Now are they Saints all in that Citie sam,
More deare vnto their God, then younglings to their dam.

Till now, said then the knight, I weened well,
    That great *Cleopolis*, where I haue beene,
    In which that fairest *Faerie Queene* doth dwell,
    The fairest Citie was, that might be seene;
    And that bright towre all built of christall cleene,
    Panthea, seemd the brightest thing, that was:
    But now by proofe all otherwise I weene;
    For this great Citie that does far surpas,
And this bright Angels towre quite dims that towre of glas.

Most trew, then said the holy aged man;
  Yet is *Cleopolis* for earthly frame,
  The fairest peece, that eye beholden can:
And well beseemes all knights of noble name,
That couet in th' immortall booke of fame
To be eternized, that same to haunt,
And doen their seruice to that soueraigne Dame,
That glorie does to them for guerdon graunt:
For she is heauenly borne, and heauen may iustly vaunt. . . .

Then seeke this path, that I to thee presage,
  Which after all to heauen shall thee send;
  Then peaceably thy painefull pilgrimage
To yonder same *Hierusalem* do bend,
Where is for thee ordaind a blessed end:
For thou emongst those Saints, whom thou doest see,
Shalt be a Saint, and thine owne nations frend
And Patrone: thou Saint *George* shalt called bee,
Saint *George* of mery England, the signe of victoree.

HENRY VAUGHAN THE SILURIST 1622–1695

from

The Pilgrimage

46. AS TRAVELLERS WHEN THE TWILIGHT'S COME

As travellers when the twilight's come,
And in the sky the stars appear,
The past day's accidents do sum
With, *Thus we saw there, and thus here.*

Then Jacob-like lodge in a place
(A place, and no more, is set down,)
Where till the day restore the race
They rest and dream homes of their own.

So for this night I linger here. . . .

from

Paradise Lost

47. THERE WAS A PLACE, NOW NOT

There was a place,
Now not, though Sin, not Time, first wraught the change,
Where *Tigris* at the foot of Paradise
Into a Gulf shot under ground, till part
Rose up a Fountain by the Tree of Life. . . .

WILLIAM COLLINS 1721–1759

from

Persian Eclogues

48. HASSAN, OR THE CAMEL DRIVER

Scene: The Desert   *Time:* Mid-day

In silent horror o'er the desert-waste
The driver Hassan with his camels past.
One cruise of water on his back he bore,
And his light scrip contain'd a scanty store:
A fan of painted feathers in his hand,
To guard his shaded face from scorching sand.
The sultry sun had gain'd the middle sky,
And not a tree, and not an herb was nigh.
The beasts, with pain, their dusty way pursue,
Shrill roar'd the winds, and dreary was the view!
With desp'rate sorrow wild th' affrighted man
Thrice sigh'd, thrice strook his breast, and thus began:
  Sad was the hour, and luckless was the day,
  When first from Shiraz' walls I bent my way.

Ah! little thought I of the blasting wind,
The thirst or pinching hunger that I find!
Bethink thee, Hassan, where shall thirst assuage,
When fails this cruise, his unrelenting rage?
Soon shall this scrip its precious load resign,
Then what but tears and hunger shall be thine?

Ye mute companions of my toils, that bear
In all my griefs a more than equal share!
Here, where no springs in murmurs break away,
Or moss-crown'd fountains mitigate the day:
In vain ye hope the green delights to know,
Which plains more blest, or verdant vales bestow.
Here rocks alone, and tasteless sands are found,
And faint and sickly winds for ever howl around.
 Sad was the hour, and luckless was the day,
 When first from Shiraz' walls I bent my way.

Curst be the gold and silver which persuade
Weak men to follow far-fatiguing trade.
The lily Peace outshines the silver store,
And life is dearer than the golden ore.
Yet money tempts us o'er the desert brown,
To ev'ry distant mart, and wealthy town:
Full oft we tempt the land, and oft the sea,
And are we only yet repay'd by thee?
Ah! why was Ruin so attractive made,
Or why fond man so easily betray'd?
Why heed we not, whilst mad we haste along,
The gentle voice of Peace, or Pleasure's song?
Or wherefore think the flow'ry mountain's side,
The fountain's murmurs, and the valley's pride,
Why think we these less pleasing to behold,
Than dreary deserts, if they lead to gold?
 Sad was the hour, and luckless was the day,
 When first from Shiraz' walls I bent my way.

O cease, my fears! all frantic as I go,
When thought creates unnumber'd scenes of woe,

What if the lion in his rage I meet!
Oft in the dust I view his printed feet:
And fearful! oft, when Day's declining light
Yields her pale empire to the mourner Night,
By hunger rous'd, he scours the groaning plain,
Gaunt wolves and sullen tigers in his train:
Before them Death with shrieks directs their way,
Fills the wild yell, and leads them to their prey.
   Sad was the hour, and luckless was the day,
   When first from Shiraz' walls I bent my way.

At that dead hour the silent asp shall creep,
If aught of rest I find, upon my sleep:
Or some swoln serpent twist his scales around,
And wake to anguish with a burning wound.
Thrice happy they, the wise contented poor,
From lust of wealth and dread of death secure;
They tempt no deserts, and no griefs they find;
Peace rules the day, where reason rules the mind.
   Sad was the hour, and luckless was the day,
   When first from Shiraz' walls I bent my way.

O hapless youth! for she thy love hath won,
The tender Zara, will be most undone!
Big swell'd my heart, and own'd the pow'rful maid,
When fast she dropt her tears, as thus she said:
'Farewell the Youth whom sighs could not detain,
Whom Zara's breaking heart implor'd in vain;
Yet as thou go'st, may ev'ry blast arise,
Weak and unfelt as these rejected sighs!
Safe o'er the wild, no perils mayst thou see,
No griefs endure, nor weep, false Youth, like me.'
O let me safely to the fair return,
Say with a kiss, she must not, shall not mourn.
Go teach my heart to lose its painful fears,
Recall'd by Wisdom's voice, and Zara's tears.

He said, and call'd on Heav'n to bless the day,
When back to Shiraz' walls he bent his way.

from

A Voice from the Nile

49. EGYPT

I come from mountains under other stars
Than those reflected in my waters here;
Athwart broad realms, beneath large skies, I flow,
Between the Libyan and Arabian hills,
And merge at last into the great Mid-Sea;
And make this land of Egypt. All is mine:
The palm-trees and the doves among the palms,
The corn-fields and the flowers among the corn,
The patient oxen and the crocodiles,
The ibis and the heron and the hawk,
The lotus and the thick papyrus reeds,
The slant-sailed boats that flit before the wind
Or up my rapids ropes hale heavily;
Yea, even all the massive temple-fronts
With all their columns and huge effigies,
The pyramids and Memnon and the Sphinx,
This Cairo and the City of the Greek
As Memphis and the hundred-gated Thebes,
Sais and Denderah of Isis queen;
Have grown because I fed them with full life,
And flourish only while I feed them still. . . .

WILFRED SCAWEN BLUNT 1840–1922

50. THE OASIS OF SIDI KHALED

How the earth burns! Each pebble underfoot
Is as a living thing with power to wound.
The white sand quivers, and the footfall mute
Of the slow camels strikes but gives no sound,
As though they walked on flame, not solid ground.
'Tis noon, and the beasts' shadows even have fled

Back to their feet, and there is fire around
And fire beneath, and overhead the sun.
Pitiful heaven! What is this we view?
Tall trees, a river, pools, where swallows fly,
Thickets of oleander where doves coo,
Shades, deep as midnight, greenness for tired eyes.
Hark, how the light winds in the palm-tops sigh.
Oh this is rest. Oh this is paradise.

PERCY BYSSHE SHELLEY 1792–1822

from
Alastor or The Spirit of Solitude

51. THE AWFUL RUINS OF THE DAYS OF OLD

His wandering step
Obedient to high thoughts, has visited
The awful ruins of the days of old:
Athens, and Tyre, and Balbec, and the waste
Where stood Jerusalem, the fallen towers
Of Babylon, the eternal pyramids,
Memphis and Thebes, and whatsoe'er of strange
Sculptured on alabaster obelisk,
Or jasper tomb, or mutilated sphynx,
Dark Æthiopia in her desert hills
Conceals. Among the ruined temples there,
Stupendous columns, and wild images
Of more than man, where marble dæmons watch
The Zodiac's brazen mystery, and dead men
Hang their mute thoughts on the mute walls around,
He lingered, poring on memorials
Of the world's youth, through the long burning day
Gazed on those speechless shapes, nor, when the moon
Filled the mysterious halls with floating shades
Suspended he that task, but ever gazed
And gazed, till meaning on his vacant mind
Flashed like strong inspiration, and he saw
The thrilling secrets of the birth of time.

from

The Modern Traveller

52. OH! AFRICA, MYSTERIOUS LAND!

To turn to more congenial topics,
    I said a little while ago
    The food was very much below
The standard needed to prepare
Explorers for the special fare
Which all authorities declare
    Is needful in the tropics.
A Frenchman sitting next to us
Rejected the asparagus;
The turtle soup was often cold,
The ices hot, the omelettes old,
The coffee worse than I can tell;
And Sin (who had a happy knack
Of rhyming rapidly and well
Like Cyrano de Bergerac)
    Said 'Quant à moi, je n'aime pas
    Du tout ce pâté de foie gras!'
But this fastidious taste
Succeeded in a startling way;
At Dinner on the following day
    They gave us Bloater Paste.
Well—hearty Pioneers and rough
    Should not be over nice;
I think these lines are quite enough,
    And hope they will suffice
To make the Caterers observe
The kind of person whom they serve.—

.   .   .   .

And yet I really must complain
About the Company's Champagne!
    This most expensive kind of wine
In England is a matter

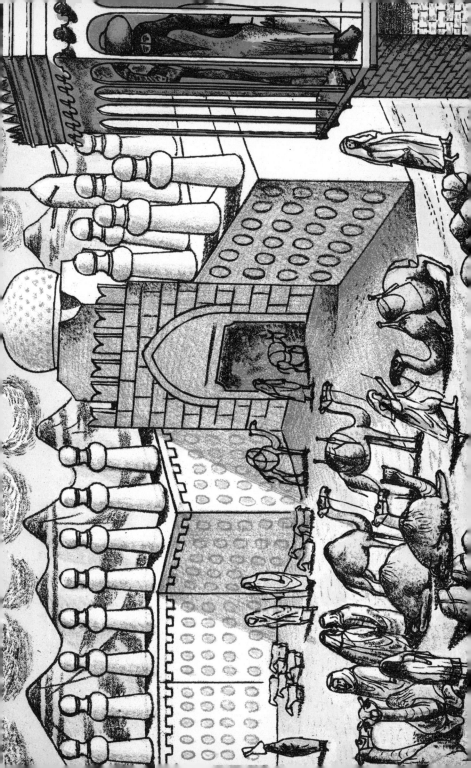

Of pride or habit when we dine
        (Presumably the latter).
Beneath an equatorial sky
You *must* consume it or you die;
And stern indomitable men
Have told me, time and time again,
'The nuisance of the tropics is
The sheer necessity of fizz.'
Consider then the carelessness—
The lack of polish and address,
        The villainy in short,
Of serving what explorers think
To be a necessary drink
In bottles holding something less
        Than one Imperial quart,
And costing quite a shilling more
Than many grocers charge ashore.

.   .   .   .   .   .

At sea the days go slipping past.
Monotonous from first to last—
A trip like any other one
In vessels going south. The sun
        Grew higher and more fiery.

We lay and drank, and swore, and played
At Trick-my-neighbour in the shade;
And you may guess how every sight,
However trivial or slight,
        Was noted in my diary.
I have it here—the usual things—
A serpent (not the sort with wings)
        Came rising from the sea:
In length (as far as we could guess)
A quarter of a mile or less.
The weather was extremely clear
The creature dangerously near
        And plain as it would be.
It had a bifurcated tail,
And in its mouth it held a whale.

Just north, I find, of Cape de Verd
We caught a very curious bird
    With horns upon its head;
And—not, as one might well suppose,
Web-footed or with jointed toes—
    But having hoofs instead.
As no one present seemed to know
Its use or name, I let it go.

On June the 7th after dark
A young and very hungry shark
    Came climbing up the side.
It ate the Chaplain and the Mate—
But why these incidents relate?
    The public must decide,
That nothing in the voyage out
Was worth their bothering about,
Until we saw the coast, which looks
Exactly as it does in books.

.   .   .   .   .

Oh! Africa, mysterious Land!
Surrounded by a lot of sand
    And full of grass and trees,
And elephants and Afrikanders,
And politics and Salamanders,
And Germans seeking to annoy,
And horrible rhinoceroi,
And native rum in little kegs,
And savages called Touaregs
    (A kind of Soudanese).
And tons of diamonds, and lots
Of nasty, dirty Hottentots,
And coolies coming from the East;
And serpents, seven yards long at least
    And lions, that retain
Their vigour, appetites and rage
Intact to an extreme old age,
    And never lose their mane.

Far Land of Ophir! Mined for gold
By lordly Solomon of old,
Who sailing northward to Perim
Took all the gold away with him,
    And left a lot of holes;
Vacuities that bring despair
    To those confiding souls
Who find that they have bought a share
In marvellous horizons, where
The Desert terrible and bare
    Interminably rolls. . . .

We beached upon a rising tide
At Saastown on the western side. . . .

In getting up our Caravan
We met a most obliging man,
The Lord Chief Justice of Liberia,
And Minister of the Interior;
Cain Abolition Beecher Boz,
Worked like a Nigger—which he was—
    And in a single day
Procured us Porters, Guides, and kit,
And would not take a sou for it
    Until we went away.*

* (But when we went away we found a deficit of several pound.)

from
The Wayzgoose

53. THE GARDEN COLONY

Attend my fable if your ears be clean,
In fair Banana Land we lay our scene—
South Africa, renowned both far and wide
For politics and little else beside:
Where, having torn the land with shot and shell,
Our sturdy pioneers as farmers dwell,
And, 'twixt the hours of strenuous sleep, relax
To shear the fleeces or to fleece the blacks:
Where every year a fruitful increase bears
Of pumpkins, cattle, sheep, and millionaires—
A clime so prosperous both to men and kine
That which were which a sage could scarce define;
Where fat white sheep upon the mountains bleat
And fatter politicians in the street;
Where lemons hang like yellow moons ashine
And grapes the size of apples load the vine;
Where apples to the weight of pumpkins go
And donkeys to the height of statesmen grow,
Where trouts the size of salmon throng the creeks
And worms the size of magistrates—the beaks;
Where the precocious tadpole, from his bog,
Becomes a journalist ere half a frog;
Where every shrimp his proud career may carve
And only brain and muscle have to starve.
The 'garden colony' they call our land,
And surely for a garden it was planned:
What apter phrase with such a place could cope
Where vegetation has so fine a scope,
Where *weeds* in such variety are found
And all the rarest *parasites* abound,
Where pumpkins to professors are promoted
And turnips into Parliament are voted?

54. NAMAQUALAND AFTER RAIN

Again the veld revives,
Imbued with lyric rains,
And sap re-sweetening dry stalks
Perfumes the quickening plains;

Small roots explode in strings of stars,
Each bulb gives up its dream,
Honey drips from orchid throats,
Jewels each raceme;

The desert sighs at dawn—
As in another hemisphere
The temple lotus breaks her buds
On the attentive air—

A frou-frou of new flowers,
Puff of unruffling petals,
While rods of sunlight strike pure streams
From rocks beveined with metals;

Far in the gaunt karroo
That winter dearth denudes,
Ironstone caves give back the burr
Of lambs in multitudes;

Grass waves again where drought
Bleached every upland kraal;
A peach-tree shoots along the wind
Pink volleys through a broken wall;

And willows growing round the dam
May now be seen
With all their traceries of twigs
Just hesitating to be green,

Soon to be hung with colonies
All swaying with the leaves
Of pendent wicker love-nests
The pretty loxia weaves.

from

Enoch Arden

55. A SHIPWRECK'D SAILOR, WAITING FOR A SAIL

The mountain wooded to the peak, the lawns
And winding glades high up like ways to Heaven,
The slender coco's drooping crown of plumes,
The lightning flash of insect and of bird,
The lustre of the long convolvuluses
That coil'd around the stately stems, and ran
Ev'n to the limit of the land, the glows
And glories of the broad belt of the world,
All these he saw; but what he fain had seen
He could not see, the kindly human face,
Nor ever hear a kindly voice, but heard
The myriad shriek of wheeling ocean-fowl,
The league-long roller thundering on the reef,
The moving whisper of huge trees that branch'd
And blossom'd in the zenith, or the sweep
Of some precipitous rivulet to the wave,
As down the shore he ranged, or all day long
Sat often in the seaward-gazing gorge,
A shipwreck'd sailor, waiting for a sail:
No sail from day to day, but every day
The sunrise broken into scarlet shafts
Among the palms and ferns and precipices;
The blaze upon the waters to the east;
The blaze upon his island overhead;
The blaze upon the waters to the west;
Then the great stars that globed themselves in Heaven,
The hollower-bellowing ocean, and again
The scarlet shafts of sunrise—but no sail.

There often as he watch'd or seem'd to watch,
So still, the golden lizard on him paused,
A phantom made of many phantoms moved
Before him haunting him, or he himself

Moved haunting people, things and places, known
Far in a darker isle beyond the line;
The babes, their babble, Annie, the small house,
The climbing street, the mill, the leafy lanes,
The peacock-yewtree and the lonely Hall,
The horse he drove, the boat he sold, the chill
November dawns and dewy-glooming downs,
The gentle shower, the smell of dying leaves,
And the low moan of leaden-colour'd seas.

ALUN LEWIS 1915-1944

56. INDIAN DAY

Dawn's cold imperative compels
Bazaars and gutters to disturb
Famine's casual ugly tableaux.
Lazarus is lifted from the kerb.

The supple sweeper girl goes by
Brushing the dung of camels from the street
The daylight's silver bangles
Glitter on her naked feet.

II

Yellow ramtilla stiffens in the noon,
Jackals skulk among the screes,
In skinny fields the oxen shiver,
The gods have prophesied disease.

Hedges of spike and rubber, hedges of cactus,
Lawns of bougainvillia, jasmine, zinnia,
Terraces of privilege and loathing,
The masterly shadows of a nightmare

Harden and grow lengthy in the drought.
The moneyed antipathetic faces
Converse in courts of pride and fountains
With ermined sleek injustices.
Gods and dacoits haunt the mountains.

III

The sun the thunder and the hunger grow
Extending stupidly the fields of pain
Ploughing the peasant under with his crop
Denying the great mercy of the rain

Denying what each flowering pear and lime
And every child and each embrace imply—
The love that is imprisoned in each heart
By the famines and fortunes of the century.

IV

Night bibles India in her wilderness
The Frontier Mail screams blazing with such terror
The russet tribesman lays aside his flute
Rigid with Time's hypnotic surging error.

The kindness of the heart lies mute
Caught in the impotence of dreams
Yet all night long the boulders sing
The timeless songs of mountain streams.

JOHN MILTON 1608–1674

from
Paradise Lost

57. HERE WALK'D THE FIEND

Here walk'd the Fiend at large in spacious field.
As when a Vultur on *Imaus* bred,
Whose snowy ridge the roving *Tartar* bounds,
Dislodging from a Region scarce of prey
To gorge the flesh of Lambs or yeanling Kids
On Hills where Flocks are fed, flies toward the Springs
Of *Ganges* or *Hydaspes*, *Indian* streams;
But in his way lights on the barren plaines
Of *Sericana*, where *Chineses* drive
With Sails and Wind thir canie Waggons light:
So on this windie Sea of Land, the Fiend
Walk'd up and down alone.

from

The Fleece

58. TRADING CARAVANS

From the proud mart of Petersburg, ere-while
The wat'ry seat of desolation wide,
Issue these trading caravans, and urge,
Through dazling snows, their dreary trackless road;
By compass steering oft, from week to week,
From month to month; whole seasons view their toils.
Neva they pass, and Kesma's gloomy flood,
Volga, and Don, and Oka's torrent prone,
Threat'ning in vain; and many a cataract,
In its fall stopp'd, and bound with bars of ice.

Close on the left unnumber'd tracts they view
White with continual frost; and on the right
The Caspian lake, and ever-flow'ry realms,
Though now abhorr'd, behind them turn, the haunt
Of arbitrary rule, where regions wide
Are destin'd to the sword; and on each hand
Roads hung with carcases, or under foot
Thick strown; while, in their rough bewilder'd vales,
The blooming rose its fragrance breathes in vain,
And silver fountains fall, and nightingales
Attune their notes, where none are left to hear.

Sometimes o'er level ways, on easy sleds,
The gen'rous horse conveys the sons of trade;
And ever and anon the docile dog;
And now the light rein-deer, with rapid pace,
Skims over icy lakes; now slow they climb
Aloft o'er clouds, and then adown descend
To hollow vallies, 'till the eye beholds
The roofs of Tobol, whose hill-crowning walls
Shine, like the rising moon, through wat'ry mists:
Tobol, th' abode of those unfortunate
Exiles of angry state, and thralls of war;

Solemn fraternity! where carl, and prince,
Soldier, and statesman, and uncrested chief,
On the dark level of adversity,
Converse familiar; while, amid the cares
And toils for hunger, thirst, and nakedness,
Their little publick smiles, and the bright sparks
Of trade are kindled. . . .

From their tenements,
Pleas'd and refresh'd, proceeds the caravan
Through lively-spreading cultures, pastures green,
And yellow tillages in op'ning woods:
Thence on, through Narim's wilds, a pathless road
They force, with rough entangling thorns perplext;
Land of the lazy Ostiacs, thin dispers'd. . . .

So on they fare,
And pass by spacious lakes, begirt with rocks,
And azure mountains; and the heights admire
Of white Imaus, whose snow-nodding craggs
Frighten the realms beneath, and from their urns
Pour mighty rivers down. . . .

These rugged paths and savage landscapes pass'd,
A new scene strikes their eyes: among the clouds
Aloft they view, what seems a chain of cliffs,
Nature's proud work; that matchless work of art,
The wall of Sina, by Chihoham's pow'r,
In earliest times, erected. Warlike troops
Frequent are seen in haughty march along
Its ridge, a vast extent, beyond the length
Of many a potent empire; tow'rs and ports,
Three times a thousand, lift thereon their brows
At equal spaces, and in prospect 'round
Cities, and plains, and kingdoms, overlook.

At length the gloomy passage they attain
Of its deep vaulted gates, whose op'ning folds
Conduct at length to Pekin's glitt'ring spires,
The destin'd mart, where joyous they arrive.

59. CHINA

The dragon hatched a cockatrice
   Cheese crumbles and not many mites repair
There is a Nature about this
   The spring and rawness tantalise the air

Most proud of being most at ease
   The sea is the most solid ground
Where comfort is on hands and knees
   The nations perch about around

Red hills bleed naked into screes—
   The classics are a single school
—The few large trees are holy trees
   They teach the nations how to rule

They will not teach the Japanese—
   They rule by music and by rites
—They are as like them as two peas
   All nations are untidy sights

The serious music strains to squeeze—
   The angel coolies sing like us
—Duties, and literature, and fees
   To lift an under-roaded bus

The paddy fields are wings of bees
   The Great Wall as a dragon crawls
To one who flies or one who sees
   The twisted contour of their walls

A liver fluke of sheep agrees
   Most rightly proud of her complacencies
With snail so well they make one picce
   Most wrecked and longest of all histories.

from

Li-Po: or The Good Governor
A Chinese Eclogue

60. LI-PO'S FAIR ISLAND

Where Honan's hills Kiansi's vale inclose,
And Xifa's lake its glassy level shows;
Li-po's fair island lay—delightful scene!
With swelling slopes, and groves of every green:
On azure rocks his rich pavilion plac'd,
Rear'd its light front with golden columns grac'd;
High o'er the roof a weeping willow hung,
And jasmine boughs the lattice twin'd among;
In porcelain vases crested amaranth grew,
And starry aster, crimson, white, and blue;
Lien-hoa flowers upon the water spread;
Bright shells and corals varied lustre shed;
From sparry grottos crystal drops distill'd
On sounding brass, and air with music fill'd;
Soft thro' the bending canes the breezes play'd,
The rustling leaves continual murmur made;
Gay shoals of gold-fish glitter'd in the tide,
And gaudy birds flew sportive by its side.
The distant prospects well the sight might please,
With pointed mountains, and romantic trees:
From craggy cliffs, between the verdant shades,
The silver rills rush'd down in bright cascades;
O'er terrac'd steeps rich cotton harvests wav'd,
And smooth canals the rice-clad valley lav'd;
Long rows of cypress parted all the land,
And tall pagodas crown'd the river's strand!

'Twas here, from business and its pomp and pain,
The pensive master sought relief in vain.
Li-po, mild prince, a viceroy's sceptre sway'd,
And ten fair towns his gentle rule obey'd. . . .

Beneath a bow'r of sweet Ka-fa, whose bloom
Fill'd all th' adjacent lawn with rich perfume,
His slaves at distance sat—a beauteous train!—
One wak'd the lute, and one the vocal strain:
They saw his brow with care all clouded o'er,
And wish'd to ease the anxiety he bore.
Amusive tales their soothing lay disclos'd,
Of heroes brave to perils strange expos'd,
Of tyrants proud, from power's high summit cast;
And lovers, long desponding, blest at last . . .
'This scene,' said he, 'how fair! to please the sight
'How Nature's charms, Art's ornaments unite!
'Those maids, what magic in the strains they sung!
'Song sweetliest flows from Beauty's tuneful tongue.
'Yet say, did Tien bid power and wealth be mine,
'For me my soul to pleasure to resign? . . .
'Think, why did Tien superior rank impart,
'Force of the mind, or feelings of the heart.
'Last night in sleep, to Fancy's sight display'd,
'Lay lovelier scenes than e'er my eyes survey'd;
'With purple shone the hills, with gold the vales,
'And greenest foliage wav'd in gentlest gales:
''Midst palmy fields, with sunshine ever bright,
'A palace rear'd its walls of silvery white;
'The gates of pearl a shady hall disclos'd,
'Where old Confucius' rev'rend form repos'd:
'Loose o'er his limbs the silk's light texture flow'd,
'His eye serene ethereal lustre show'd:
"My son," said he, as near his seat I drew,
"Cast round this wonderous spot thy dazzled view;
"See how, by lucid founts in myrtle bowers,
"The blest inhabitants consume their hours!
"They ne'er to War, fell Fiend! commission gave
"To murder, ravage, banish, and enslave;
"They ne'er bid Grandeur raise her gorgeous pile,
"With tribute ravish'd from the hand of Toil;
"But parents, guardians of the people reign'd,
"The weak defended, and the poor sustain'd."
'Smiling he ceas'd—the vision seem'd to fly,
'Like fleecy clouds dispersing in the sky.

85

'Arise, Li-po! and cast thy robes aside,
'Disguise thy form, thy well-known features hide;
'Go forth, yon streets, yon crowded streets pervade,
'Mix with the throng, and mark who seeks thy aid. . . .'

He spoke, and rose; but now along the way
That from the city-gate fair-winding lay,
Stretch'd thro' green meads where lowing cattle graz'd,
Amid the lake's wide silver level rais'd,
Led up steep rocks by painted bridges join'd,
Or near thin trees that o'er the tide inclin'd,
Slow tow'rds his palace came a suppliant train;—
Whoe'er his presence sought ne'er sought in vain—
The ready vessel, waiting at his call,
Receiv'd, and bore him to the audience-hall.

WALTER JAMES TURNER b. 1889

from

The Shepherd goes to War

61. AUSTRALIAN SHEPHERD

The days, the years, half life slips by
Under that bright Australian sky:
The gum trees are a rustling dream
Upon the sunshine's golden stream:

The whip-bird and the cockatoo,
They are the cries of dream-birds too,
And more unearthly and unreal
Grows Kookaburra's mocking peal.

Still-magic is the country round,
Dead branches strew the snake-bright ground:
In luminous transparency
Quivers each thin-leaved, blue-green tree:

There is an ecstasy of light;
And Silence is as lightning bright:
The earthflower, air, a still, blue blaze
Springs from earth's pot those rainless days.

The Shepherd sees as in a glass
The flitting lyre-birds soundless pass,
The Trees in sunlight standing deep,
A world in an enchanted sleep.

PADRAIC COLUM b. 1881

62. HAWAII

Not in a grove where each tree loses its presence, not singly, do
Lehua trees grow; they are Lehua trees only when they grow as I
saw them growing at Kapaho, on Hawaii.

When I had seen them before they were mingled with other trees,
or they grew singly, a tree here and a tree there: looking upon them
I had marvelled that the poets of Hawaii had emblemed their
warriors as Lehua trees. . . .

But in Kapaho, on Hawaii, they stand upon lava rock and upon
lava crust; some like mighty champions, like Kamehameha, like Umi,
stand upon high places, upon mounds and rocks of lava. All stand
in ranks as if all the warriors of the Eight Islands stood spear-ready
upon that lava waste.

With branches from the ground they grow. From top to bottom the
blossoms show themselves—not blossoms but the precious ornaments
the warrior decks himself with.

The blossoms show themselves amongst the leaves; they are like
scarlet birds, the lost i-i-wi birds, come back to hide and show themselves in the trees beloved of Hiiaka.

They stand upon the lava waste, upon black rocks and amongst
black shingles; rank upon rank they grow, like warriors standing
erect in the red glow of the volcano.

I saw your lava-mounting trees, and I marvelled no more that your poets had emblemed your warriors as Lehua trees. . . .

They have departed, the warriors whom these trees emblemed. Honey for the birds of Heaven, wreaths of red for girls to deck their lovers with—these your Lehua trees still bring out of your fire-formed rock, Hawaii.

JAMES THOMSON 1700–1748

from
The Seasons

63. THE MIGHTY ORELLANA

Swelled by a thousand streams, impetuous hurled
From all the roaring Andes, huge descends
The mighty Orellana. Scarce the muse
Dares stretch her wing o'er this enormous mass
Of rushing water; scarce she dares attempt
The sea-like Plata, to whose dread expanse,
Continuous depth, and wondrous length of course
Our floods are rills. With unabated force
In silent dignity they sweep along,
And traverse realms unknown, and blooming wilds,
And fruitful deserts—worlds of solitude
Where the sun smiles and seasons teem in vain,
Unseen and unenjoyed. Forsaking these,
O'er peopled plains they far-diffusive flow
And many a nation feed, and circle safe
In their soft bosom many a happy isle,
The seat of blameless Pan, yet undisturbed
By Christian crimes and Europe's cruel sons.
Thus pouring on they proudly seek the deep,
Whose vanquish'd tide, recoiling from the shock,
Yields to this liquid weight of half the globe;
And Ocean trembles for his green domain.

from

De Guiana Carmen Epicum

64. GUIANA

Guiana, whose rich feet are mines of gold,
Whose forehead knocks against the roof of stars,
Stands on her tip-toes at fair England looking,
Kissing her hand, bowing her mighty breast,
And every sign of all submission making,
To be her sister and the daughter both
Of our most sacred Maid. . . .

SIR WALTER RALEGH C. 1552–1618

from

The Book of the Ocean to Cynthia

65. RALEGH TO QUEEN ELIZABETH

To seek new worlds, for gold, for praise, for glory,
　To try desire, to try love severed far,
When I was gone she sent her memory,
　More strong than were ten thousand ships of war,

To call me back, to leave great honour's thought,
　To leave my friends, my fortune, my attempt,
To leave the purpose I so long had sought,
　And hold both cares and comforts in contempt.

Such heat in ice, such fire in frost remained,
　Such trust in doubt, such comfort in despair;
Much like the gentle lamb, though lately weaned,
　Plays with the dug, though finds no comfort there.

But as a body violently slain
    Retaineth warmth although the spirit be gone,
And by a power in nature moves again,
    Till it be laid below the fatal stone;

Or as the earth, even in cold winter days
    Left for a time by her life-giving sun,
Doth by the power remaining of his rays
    Produce some green, though not as it hath done;

Or as a wheel, forced by the falling stream,
    Although the course be turned some other way,
Doth for a time go round upon the beam,
    Till, wanting strength to move, it stands at stay;

So my forsaken heart, my withered mind,
    Widow of all the joys it once possessed,
My hopes clean out of sight with forced wind
    To kingdoms strange, to lands far-off addressed,

Alone, forsaken, friendless, on the shore,
    With many wounds, with death's cold pangs embraced,
Writes in the dust, as one that could no more,
    Whom love, and time, and fortune had defaced,

Of things so great, so long, so manifold,
    With means so weak, the soul even then departing
The weal, the woe, the passages of old,
    And worlds of thoughts described by one last scything.

As if when after Phoebus is descended
    And leaves a light much like the past day's dawning,
And, every toil and labour wholly ended,
    Each living creature draweth to his resting,

We should begin by such a parting light
    To write the story of all ages past,
And end the same before th' approaching night.

Such is again the labour of my mind,
    Whose shroud, by sorrow woven now to end,
Hath seen that ever shining sun declined,
    So many years that so could not descend,

But that the eyes of my mind held her beams
    In every part transferred by love's swift thought;
Far off or near, in waking or in dreams,
    Imagination strong their lustre brought.

Such force her angel-like appearance had
    To master distance, time, or cruelty,
Such art to grieve, and after to make glad,
    Such fear in love, such love in majesty.

My weary limbs her memory embalmed;
    My darkest ways her eyes made clear as day.
What storms so great but Cynthia's beams appeased?
    What rage so fierce, that love could not allay?

Twelve years entire I wasted in this war,
    Twelve years of my most happy younger days;
But I in them, and they now wasted are,
    'Of all which past the sorrow only stays'.

MATTHEW GREGORY ('MONK') LEWIS 1775–1818

66. THE TROPIC GENIUS

What triumph moves on the billows so blue?
In his car of pellucid pearl I view,
With glorious pomp, on the dancing tide,
The tropic Genius proudly ride.

The flying fish, who trail his car,
Dazzle the eye, as they shine from afar;
Twinkling their fins in the sun, and show
All the hues which adorn the showery bow.

Of dark sea-blue is the mantle he wears;
For a sceptre a plantain branch he bears;
Pearls his sable arms surround,
And his locks of wool with coral are crown'd.

Perpetual sunbeams round him stream;
His bronzed limbs shine with golden gleam;
The spicy spray from his wheels that showers,
Makes the sense ache with its odorous powers.

Myriads of monsters, who people the caves
Of ocean, attendant plough the waves;
Sharks and crocodiles bask in his blaze,
And whales spout the waters which dance in his rays.

And as onward floats that triumph gay,
The light sea-breezes around it play;
While at his royal feet lie bound
The Ouragans, hush'd in sleep profound.

Dark Genius, hear a stranger's prayer,
Nor suffer those winds to ravage and tear
Jamaica's savannas, and loose to fly,
Mingling the earth, and the sea, and the sky.

From thy locks on my harvest of sweets diffuse,
To swell my canes, refreshing dews;
And kindly breathe, with cooling powers,
Through my coffee walks and shaddock bowers.

Let not thy strange diseases prey
On my life; but scare from my couch away
The yellow Plague's imps; and safe let me rest
From that dread black demon, who racks the breast:

Nor force my throbbing temples to know
Thy sunbeam's sudden and maddening blow;
Nor bid thy day-flood blaze too bright
On nerves so fragile, and brain so light:

And let me, returning in safety, view
Thy triumph again on the ocean blue;
And in Britain I'll oft with flowers entwine
The Tropic Sovereign's ebony shrine!

Was it but fancy? did He not frown,
And in anger shake his coral crown?
Gorgeous and slow the pomp moves on!
Low sinks the sun—and all is gone!

JOHN DRYDEN 1631–1700

from

The Indian Emperor

67. WHERE GOLDEN ORE LIES MIXT WITH COMMON SAND

Scene—*A pleasant Indian Country*

Enter Cortez, Vasquez, Pizarro, with Spaniards and Indians
in their party

Cortez: On what new happy climate are we thrown,
So long kept secret, and so lately known;
As if our old world modestly withdrew,
And here, in private, had brought forth a new?

Vasquez: Corn, wine, and oil, are wanting to this ground,
In which our countries fruitfully abound:
As if this infant world, yet unarrayed,
Naked and bare, in Nature's lap were laid.
No useful arts have yet found footing here;
But all untaught and salvage does appear.

Cortez: Wild and untaught are terms which we alone
Invent, for fashions differing from our own;
For all their customs are by nature wrought,
But we, by art, unteach what nature taught.

Pizarro: In Spain, our springs, like old men's children be
Decay'd and wither'd from their infancy:

93

No kindly showers fall on our barren earth,
To hatch the seasons in a timely birth.
Our summer such a russet livery wears,
As in a garment often dy'd appears.

Cortez: Here nature spreads her fruitful sweetness round,
Breaths on the air and broods upon the ground.
Here days and nights the only seasons be,
The sun no climate does so gladly see:
When forc'd from hence, to view our parts, he mourns,
Takes little journeys, and makes quick returns.

Vasquez: Methinks we walk in dreams on fairy land,
Where golden ore lies mixt with common sand;
Each downfall of a flood, the mountains pour
From their rich bowels, rolls a silver shower.

Cortez: Heaven from all ages wisely did provide
This wealth, and for the bravest nation hide,
Who with four hundred foot and forty horse,
Dare boldly go a new found world to force.

Pizarro: Our men, though valiant, we should find too few,
But Indians join the Indians to subdue;
Taxallan, shook by Montezuma's powers,
Has, to resist his forces, call'd in ours.

Vasquez: Rashly to arm against so great a king,
I hold not safe, nor is it just to bring
A war, without a fair defiance made.

Pizarro: Declare we first our quarrel: then invade.

Cortez: Myself, my king's ambassador will go;
Speak, Indian guide, how far to Mexico?

Indian: Your eyes can scarce so far a prospect make,
As to discern the city on the lake;
But that broad caus-way will direct your way,
And you may reach the town by noon of day.

Cortez: Command a party of our Indians out,
With a strict charge, not to engage, but scout:
By noble ways we conquest will prepare;
First, offer peace, and that refus'd make war.

94

from
Ruth

68. GEORGIA

He spake of plants that hourly change
Their blossoms, through a boundless range
Of intermingling hues;
With budding, fading, faded flowers
They stand the wonder of the bowers
From morn to evening dews.

He told of the magnolia, spread
High as a cloud, high over head!
The cypress and her spire;
—Of flowers that with one scarlet gleam
Cover a hundred leagues, and seem
To set the hills on fire.

The Youth of green savannahs spake,
And many an endless, endless lake,
With all its fairy crowds
Of islands, that together lie
As quietly as spots of sky
Among the evening clouds.

GEORGE BERKELEY BISHOP OF CLOYNE 1684–1753

69. ON THE PROSPECT OF PLANTING ARTS AND LEARNING IN AMERICA

The Muse, disgusted at an age and clime
Barren of every glorious theme,
In distant lands now waits a better time,
Producing subjects worthy fame:

In happy climes, where from the genial sun
   And virgin earth such scenes ensue,
The force of art by nature seems outdone,
   And fancied beauties by the true:.

In happy climes the seat of innocence,
   Where nature guides and virtue rules,
Where men shall not impose for truth and sense
   The pedantry of courts and schools:

There shall be sung another golden age,
   The rise of empire and of arts,
The good and great inspiring epic rage,
   The wisest heads and noblest hearts.

Not such as *Europe* breeds in her decay;
   Such as she bred when fresh and young,
When heavenly flame did animate her clay,
   By future poets shall be sung.

Westward the course of empire takes its way;
   The four first acts already past,
A fifth shall close the drama with the day;
   Time's noblest offspring is the last.

ARCHIBALD MacLEISH b. 1892

70. COLLOQUY FOR THE STATES

There's talk says Illinois.
                        Is there says Iowa.
There's talk on the east wind says Illinois.
Talk about what says Dakota says Kansas says Arkansas.
Can't make out: too far east says Michigan.
East of the roosters says Indiana.
                     East of the
Morning crows says Ohio.
                     East says York State.
East still says Connecticut: on east.

It's down east from here says Massachusetts.
It's east of the Quoddy says Maine but I hear it.
                              Hear
What says Texas.
                    What can you hear says Virginia.
Can't be sure says Maine. Surf on the reefs.
Ice pounding away on the pans in Penobscot.
Listen says Oregon.
                        Scoop your ear says Kentucky.
Can't tell says Maine. Too much fog.
Bells on the Old Orchard. Horns at Ogunquit.
Listen says Mississippi.
                        Try to says Texas.
Lean your lug to the loo'ard says Massachusetts.
It's tall talk says Maine. It's tall talking—
Tall as a calf in a fog.
                        Call it says Arkansas.
It's mean talk says Maine. It's mouthy meaning.
Mean about what says Nebraska.
                        Mean about us.
What about us says Kentucky says Texas says Idaho.
I gather they don't like us says Maine.
                              Do
Tell says Connecticut.
                    I vum says New Hampshire.
I gather we've low ways says Maine.
                        That
So says Kansas.
                        Take my seat says Michigan.
It's how we marry says Maine. We ain't choosers.
We scrabble them up and we mingle them in. We marry the
Irish girls with the shoes with the quick come-after.
We marry the Spaniards with the evening eyes.
We marry the English with the tiptoe faces.
We marry the golden Swedes: the black Italians:
The German girls with the thick knees: the Mexicans
Lean and light in the sun with the jingling and jangling:
The Chileñas for luck: the Jews for remembrance: the Scots girls.
Tall as a tall man—silver as salmon:
The French with the skilful fingers: the long loves.

I gather we marry too many says Maine: too various.
I gather we're bad blood: we're mixed people.

That's what they say says Texas.
                    That's what they're saying.
What's in their soup says Arkansas: what they been eating?
What's in their hair says Maryland.
                    Aren't they men:
Can't they make it with strangers says Alabama.
Are they shy says Missouri.
                    Or what says Montana.
                    I gather they're
Bred pure says Maine: They're superior people.
Have they seen our kids says York State: the tall girls
The small elegant breasts they have like Egyptians
The long legs with the delicate slender bones
And the wrists supple and small as a man's three fingers—
The way they walk on the world with their narrow heels?
You can tell them anywhere: tell them in any country—
The height of their heads and the tilt of their heels when they walk:
A head higher than most: a hand smaller.
Have they raced our boys says Michigan—fast as black snakes:
Quick on the gun as quail: the sweet striders:
The watchful lads in the lead: dangerous followers:
Strong hearts in the stretch home. Have they beaten them?
I gather they haven't says Maine. I gather we're mixed
Bloods: they don't take to us.
                    Don't they says Kansas.
Have they seen our towns says Kansas: seen our wheat:
Seen our flat cars in the Rocky Mountains:
Seen our four-lane highways: seen our planes
Silver over the Alleghenies the Lakes
The big timber the tall corn the horses—
Silver over the snow-line: over the surf?
Have they seen our farms says Kansas: and who ploughed them?
Have they seen our towns says Kansas: and who planned them?
Have they seen our men says Kansas.
                    Gather not:
Gather we're bad blood says Maine. They're saying so.
Who says says Missouri: who's this saying?

Where from says Montana: where's he from?
Where from: who says Georgia.

                            Can't make out.
Way east: east of the Rhine it might be.
The wind veers says Maine. I don't make out.

East of the Rhine: so that's it says Montana.
The pure-bloods by the Rhine says Carolina.
The blood we left behind us says Wisconsin.
The blood we left behind us when we left:
The blood afraid of travel says Nevada.
The blood afraid of changes says Kentucky.
The blood afraid of strangers says Vermont:—
Strange stars and strange women: the two of them.
The blood that never hankered for a strange one:—
A dark one says Dakota with strange hair.
Stayed home and married their kin says Missouri.
Married their cousins who looked like their mothers says Michigan.
So that's all: east of the Rhine says Wisconsin.
So that's all says Arkansas: all for that—
All for the pure-blood boys afraid of strangers.

Surf on the reefs says Maine: ice on Penobscot. . . .
There's talk says Iowa.

                         Talk says Illinois.
Bells on the Old Orchard: bells at Ogunquit. . . .

Clash of corn in the wind says Illinois.

EDWARD THOMPSON 1886–1946

71. EAST RIVER, BROOKLYN

The River glares with green and crimson eyes,
And, like the monster-haunted Amazon,
Bellows and groans from alligator-throat.
Night passes. And Manhattan's mountains rise
Pale in the pearl-white dawn—chaste calm remote.
The lurid blatant beast with dark has gone.

72. CAPE ANN

O quick quick quick, quick hear the song-sparrow,
Swamp-sparrow, fox-sparrow, vesper-sparrow
At dawn and dusk. Follow the dance
Of the goldfinch at noon. Leave to chance
The Blackburnian warbler, the shy one. Hail
With shrill whistle the note of the quail, the bob-white
Dodging by bay-bush. Follow the feet
Of the walker, the water-thrush. Follow the flight
Of the dancing arrow, the purple martin. Greet
In silence the bullbat. All are delectable. Sweet sweet sweet
But resign this land at the end, resign it
To its true owner, the tough one, the sea-gull.
The palaver is finished.

ANONYMOUS

from
The Greenland Fishery

73. AND FOR ENGLAND BEAR AWAY

'The winter star doth now appear,
　　So, boys, the anchor weigh;
'Tis time to leave this cold country,
　　And for England bear away, brave boys!
　　And for England bear away.

'For Greenland is a barren place,
　　A land where grows no green,
But ice and snow, and the whale-fish blow,
　　And the daylight's seldom seen, brave boys!
　　And the daylight's seldom seen!'

74. GUNNAR'S HOWE ABOVE THE HOUSE AT LITHEND

Ye who have come o'er the sea
to behold this grey minster of lands,
Whose floor is the tomb of time past,
and whose walls by the toil of dead hands
Show pictures amidst of the ruin
of deeds that have overpast death,
Stay by this tomb in a tomb
to ask of who lieth beneath.
Ah! the world changeth too soon,
that ye stand there with unbated breath,
As I name him that Gunnar of old,
who erst in the haymaking tide
Felt all the land fragrant and fresh,
as amidst of the edges he died.
Too swiftly fame fadeth away,
if ye tremble not lest once again
The grey mound should open and show him
glad-eyed without grudging or pain.
Little labour methinks to behold him
but the tale-teller laboured in vain.
Little labour for ears that may hearken
to hear his death-conquering song,
Till the heart swells to think of the gladness
undying that overcame wrong.
O young is the world yet meseemeth
and the hope of it flourishing green,
When the words of a man unremembered
so bridge all the days that have been,
As we look round about on the land
that these nine hundred years he hath seen.

Dusk is abroad on the grass
of this valley amidst of the hill:
Dusk that shall never be dark
till the dawn hard on midnight shall fill

The trench under Eyiafell's snow,
and the grey plain the sea meeteth grey.
White, high aloft hangs the moon
that no dark night shall brighten ere day,
For here day and night toileth the summer
lest deedless his time pass away.

FRANCIS QUARLES 1592–1644

from
Argalus and Parthenia

75. BEHOLD THE HARBOUR'S NEAR

Sail gentle pinnace: now the heavens are clear,
The winds blow fair: behold the harbour's near,
Tridented Neptune hath forgot to frown,
The rocks are past: the storm is over-blown.
Up weather-beaten voyagers, and rouse ye,
Forsake your loathed cabins: up and louse ye
Upon the open decks, and smell the land:
Cheer up: the welcome shore is nigh at hand:
Sail gentle pinnace, with a prosperous gale,
To th' Isle of Peace: sail, gentle pinnace, sail:
Fortune conduct thee! Let thy keel divide
The silver streams, that thou mayst safely slide
Into the bosom of thy quiet quay,
And quit thee fairly of th' injurious sea.

from

Adventures of Richard

76. PERMIT ME OF THESE UNKNOWN LANDS
T' INQUIRE

The Brothers dined, and with that plenteous fare
That seldom fails to dissipate our care,
At least the lighter kind; and oft prevails
When reason, duty, nay, when kindness fails.
Yet food and wine, and all that mortals bless,
Lead them to think of peril and distress;
Cold, hunger, danger, solitude, and pain,
That men in life's adventurous ways sustain.
    'Thou hast sail'd far, dear brother,' said the 'squire—
'Permit me of these unknown lands t' inquire,
Lands never till'd, where thou hast wandering been,
And all the marvels thou hast heard and seen:
Do tell me something of the miseries felt
In climes where travellers freeze, and where they melt;
And be not nice,—we know 'tis not in men,
Who travel far, to hold a steady pen:
Some will, 'tis true, a bolder freedom take,
And keep our wonder always wide awake;
We know of those whose dangers far exceed
Our frail belief, that trembles as we read;
Such as in deserts burn, and thirst, and die,
Save a last gasp that they recover by:
Then, too, their hazard from a tyrant's arms,
A tiger's fury, or a lady's charms;
Besides th' accumulated evils borne
From the bold outset to the safe return.
These men abuse; but thou hast fair pretence
To modest dealing, and to mild good sense;
Then let me hear thy struggles and escapes
In the far lands of crocodiles and apes:
Say, hast thou, Bruce-like, knelt upon the bed
Where the young Nile uplifts his branchy head?

Or been partaker of th' unhallow'd feast,
Where beast-like man devours his fellow beast,
And churn'd the bleeding life? while each great dame
And sovereign beauty bade adieu to shame?
Or did the storm, that thy wreck'd pinnace bore
Impel thee gasping on some unknown shore;
Where, when thy beard and nails were savage grown,
Some swarthy princess took thee for her own,
Some danger-dreading Yarico, who, kind,
Sent thee away, and, prudent, staid behind?
  'Come—I am ready wonders to receive,
Prone to assent, and willing to believe.'
  Richard replied: 'It must be known, to you,
That tales improbable may yet be true;
And yet it is a foolish thing to tell
A tale that shall be judged improbable;
While some impossibilities appear
So like the truth, that we assenting hear.'

WILFRED SCAWEN BLUNT 1840–1922

from
'*Sed nos qui vivimus*'

77. HE TELLS OF HIS TRAVELS

Tales of great mountains where he set his steps in early manhood,
  Not hills like ours, but craggy pinnacles that pierce the clouds,
Abysmal valleys and white slopes of treacherous ice, whose foothold
  Failed as in dreams men fail and urged him headlong down,

Falling for ever—ever—and yet saved by intervention,
  On the extreme curve's edge, of a miraculous softer snow,
Wherein he bedded lay with beating heart till the slow rescue
  Gravely descending came and bore him scathless home;

Or of the unlimited fields revealed of grey Arabian desert,
　Where are no streams or shade, but only the blind haze of noon,
And the sun strikes with might, and the skins shrink which hold his
　　blessing,
　The dole of water spared, his forfeit life if these be gone;

Drear and untenanted. Yet see the sudden transformation
　When the Spring rains have come! In every vale and hollow there
Cattle unnumbered pasture knee-deep down in purple blossoms,
　And the calf-camels prance, and their dams roar like souls in pain.

Or of days spent alone and nights in far Brazilian forests,
　Where sky and earth itself are lost in insolent depths of green.
High overhead the laden tree-tops touch the extremest heaven,
　Leading through latticed walls of flowers and veils deep-dripped
　　with dew.

The impenetrable shadows dark of that shut place of silence
　How are they broken by the sheen and glint of insect wings,
Bright coloured lamps slow flitting! Lo from the impervious thicket
　A blaze of blue, a butterfly, bursts flashing through the trees.

Or last, of the vast hum of a tumultuous Indian city,
　Where street and bridge are thronged with men who sell and buy
　　and cry,
And women with bright eyes half veiled pass, bearing flowers and
　　incense,
　Through the tall temple gates set wide, to gods in ochreous shrines.

JOHN KENYON 1784–1856

78. THE TRAVELLED OYSTER

　　An oyster, upon oozy bed,
　　Like his forefathers, born and bred,
　　It chanced, was wafted far and wide
　　By force of wind and force of tide;
　　Nor are there wanting folk to say

He drifted fairly round the bay.
At last he drifted back agen;
The very finest one might ken
Of travelled oyster-gentlemen.
For, though ne'er out of his own shell,
He saw, or thought he saw, as well,
And was, or deemed himself, as wise
As fishes who use fins and eyes.
In secret news he yields to none;
Knows all the deeds by mussels done;
'Mong limpets what dark plots are hatching,
What territory prawns are snatching;
And has—from information—glimpse
Of coming war among the shrimps.
On all who hap within his reach,
(For 'tis his darling pride to teach)
He rolls that tongue which none may quell;
While every brother of the shell
Is sadly bound to stand the shock,
Chained, like Prometheus, to his rock.

And, Reader! we have seen, I wis,
Full many a dull-brained fish like this,
Who, having drifted Europe round,
Floats back at last to his old ground;
And though, like oyster, shut within
His sulky shell, he nought hath seen,
Yet still, in right of foreign travel,
Assumes to talk—instruct and cavil.
Speak of a church—he quotes Saint Peter's;
A watch—he cites Breguet's repeaters;
And e'en the trout, on which we dine,
Would have been better from the Rhine;
While we, chair-bound and wretched quite,
Are forced to feign a mien polite.

Good Reader! were it ours to choose,
Such ne'er should quit their native ooze;
Or ne'er, at least, should hit the track
Which brings them, for our torture, back.

79. CONVERSATION

*Supposed to be held between Mr. R., Mrs. R., Miss R., and Master R.,
on New Year's morning, 1836*

Mr. R.:   What a time,—nearly nine!

Miss R.:   Breakfast's been a long time ready.

Mrs. R.:   What a wind from behind!
Mary can't have shut the door.
It is open, I am sure.
Go and shut it
Quickly.

Miss R.:   But it,
Ma'am, is shut already.

Mrs. R.:   Is it close? I suppose,
Then, it's something in the kitchen,—
Windows open,—doors ajar.
Lucy, Lucy! go and do see!

Lucy: Ma'am, there an't.

Mrs. R.:   I'm sure there are.

Mr. R.:   You don't expect that at this time it
Can be any better!
Climate, climate,—only climate!
This is English weather!
Sharply here the winters close in;
Here you know we can't complain
Of cold severe.

Master R.:   Ponds all frozen!

Miss R.:   Hail and snow!

Master R.:   Wind and rain!

Mr. R.:   Glass and bones all brittle! I
               Vex myself with thinking how
               Fine the weather may be now
               Far away in Italy.

Master R.: Sky so blue over you!

Miss R.:   Moon so bright in the night!

Mr. R.:   *There* come neither clouds nor storm;

Master R.: But lovely weather,

Miss R.:   Mild and warm.

Mrs. R.:   Ay, and poison in the air!
               Better here than anywhere,—
               Sitting at the breakfast-table,
               Reading in your easy-chair.
               All your party
               Strong and hearty,
               Gathered round a cheerful fire
               Warmly blazing:—
               'Tis amazing
               That you grumble constantly!
               Pray, what more would you desire?

Mr. R.:   Softer air and sunnier sky,
               And a clime where no one knows
               What it is to blow one's nose.
               Ever since the Alps we crossed
               —'Twas indeed a piece of folly—
               We've been really tempest-tossed—

               Drenched with rain and pinched with frost.
               Then the town's so melancholy!
               People come for hours to chatter
               Over every little matter;—
               My prices and my wine run down,—
               This too pale, and that's too brown.—

Mrs. R.:   Yet they come in every day for it,
               And you know you make them pay for it!

Mr. R. (without noticing the interruption):

> There behind my desk sit I,
> Writing letters dull and dry;
> Or in the docks, I stand and shiver,
> In the damp air of the river;
> Or in the docks where mingled are
> Sawdust, cobwebs, oil and tar;
> Or on the quay, when London fog sheds
> A yellow light on butts and hogsheads,
> 'Mid vessels, anchors, ropes, and bowsprits,—
> I often find myself in low spirits.
> And in the midst of it all, I
> Think how very different
> Were my employments when we went
> Travelling in Italy;—
> Seeing churches, large and fair,—

Master R.: Gems and marbles, rich and rare,—

Miss R.: Palaces, of pictures quite full,—

Mr. R.: Lakes and mountains,—

Master R.:   Oh, delightful!

Mr. R.: Distant Alps, and handsome cities;
> Is it not a thousand pities
> That we are not there?

Mrs. R.: No, indeed! I wonder to hear you!
> Don't you know, my dear, that here you
> Have the same thing every day,
> After getting through the first of it?

Mr. R.: Is not that just what I say?
> That's the very worst of it!
> Not change, indeed! I wish it would!

Mrs. R.: I never knew a man so rude:
> You interrupt so! Here, I say,
> You stoutly keep the cold at bay;
> But there, on whistling wings the wind blows
> Through cracking walls and open windows,
> Bringing o'er the Adriatic,

To the tourist so ecstatic,
Colds, catarrhs, and pains rheumatic;
Or Sirocco from Morocco,
With its poison-heated breath,
Blows across the panting plain
Cholera, and plague, and death.
'Twould be an improvement, truly,
On the cold that ends our year,
If you'd take the cold more coolly,—
Spring will soon be here!

Mr. R. (*after a pause of reflection*):

Travelling, I must allow,
Sometimes is a little cloying;
And has inconveniences,
Though perhaps they are not great,—
Rising early, riding late,—
Also, notes of one's expenses,
Which I always find annoying.
And though a wish for sunnier skies
Sometimes in one's mind will rise,
Vexing one a little, I
Think that one may spend as gay
A Christmas or a New-Year's-Day
In England, as in Italy!

RUDYARD KIPLING 1865–1936

80. JOBSON'S AMEN

'Blessèd be the English and all their ways and works.
Cursèd be the Infidels, Hereticks, and Turks!'
'Amen,' quo' Jobson, 'but where I used to lie
Was neither Candle, Bell nor Book to curse my brethren by:

'But a palm-tree in full bearing, bowing down, bowing down,
To a surf that drove unsparing at the brown-walled town,—
Conches in a temple, oil-lamps in a dome—
And a low moon out of Africa said: "This way home!"'

'Blessèd be the English and all that they profess.
Cursèd be the Savages that prance in nakedness!'
'Amen,' quo' Jobson, 'but where I used to lie
Was neither shirt nor pantaloons to catch my brethren by:

'But a well-wheel slowly creaking, going round, going round,
By a water-channel leaking over drowned, warm ground—
Parrots very busy in the trellised pepper-vine—
And a high sun over Asia shouting: "Rise and shine!"'

'Blessèd be the English and everything they own.
Cursèd be the Infidels that bow to wood and stone!'
'Amen,' quo' Jobson, 'but where I used to lie
Was neither pew nor Gospelleer to save my brethren by:

'But a desert stretched and stricken, left and right, left and right,
Where the piled mirages thicken under white-hot light—
A skull beneath a sand-hill and a viper coiled inside—
And a red wind out of Libya roaring: "Run and hide!"'

'Blessèd be the English and all they make or do.
Cursèd be the Hereticks who doubt that this is true!'
'Amen,' quo' Jobson, 'but where I mean to die
Is neither rule nor calliper to judge the matter by:

'But Himàlya heavenward-heading, sheer and vast, sheer and vast,
In a million summits bedding on the last world's past—
A certain sacred mountain where the scented cedars climb,
And—the feet of my Belovèd hurrying back through Time!'

MATTHEW PRIOR 1664–1721

81. WRITTEN AT PARIS 1700, IN THE BEGINNING OF ROBE'S GEOGRAPHY

Of all that William rules, or Robe
Describes, great Rhea, of thy globe;
When or on post-horse, or in chaise,
With much expence, and little ease,

My destin'd miles I shall have gone,
By Thames or Maas, by Po or Rhone,
And found no foot of earth my own;
Great Mother, let me once be able
To have a garden, house, and stable;
That I may read, and ride, and plant,
Superior to desire, or want;
And as health fails, and years increase,
Sit down, and think, and die in peace.
Oblige thy fav'rite undertakers
To throw me in but twenty acres:
This number sure they may allow;
For pasture ten, and ten for plough:
'Tis all that I wou'd wish, or hope,
For me, and John, and Nell, and Crop.

Then, as thou wil't, dispose the rest
(And let not Fortune spoil the jest)
To those, who at the market-rate
Can barter honour for estate.

Now if thou grant'st me my request,
To make thy vot'ry truly blest,
Let curst revenge, and saucy pride,
To some bleak rock far off be ty'd;
Nor e'er approach my rural seat,
To tempt me to be base, and great.
And, Goddess, this kind office done,
Charge Venus to command her son,
(Wherever else she lets him rove)
To shun my house, and field, and grove:
Peace cannot dwell with hate or love.

Hear, gracious Rhea, what I say:
And thy petitioner shall pray.

NOTES AND ACKNOWLEDGEMENTS

Reference is to the *Numbers*, not to pages

1. From *Gryll Grange*, Ch. xxvii. *Fraser's Magazine*, 1860; in book form, 1861
2. From Part II, 56, 1934. Reprinted by courtesy of the Author and Faber & Faber, Ltd.
3. From *Prosopopoia: or Mother Hubberd's Tale*, lines 83–90. *Complaints*, including *Mother Hubberd* 1591
4. See *Samuel Daniel, Poems and A Defence of Ryme*, ed. A. C. Sprague, Harvard, 1930. *Ulysses and the Siren* appeared in *Certaine Small Poems*, 1605
5. A translation of the Castilian ballad. Included in *Collected Poems*, 1916. Reprinted by courtesy of J. M. Dent & Sons
6. III, 540–551
7. Printed 1633
8. Printed by E. H. Coleridge, from a manuscript dated 1824. *Complete Poetical Works*, Clarendon Press, 1912, I, 443–447, where it is stated that 'it was probably written for and may have been published in a newspaper or periodical'
9. I, i, 11–18
10. Canto II, stanza xii. See Nos. 21 and 22 and Notes
11. From *Complete Works*, ed. W. G. Sendall, 1918. (*Dover to Munich* is not anthologized here in its entirety.) Included in *Verses and Translations*, first published 1861
12. This *Winter-Piece* appeared in *The Tatler*, No. 12, 7 May 1709, and was afterwards revised. Ambrose Philips, Miss Segar tells us, was in Denmark in 1708–9, as Secretary to the British Envoy, Daniel Pulteney. The Earl of Dorset to whom the epistle is addressed was the Seventh Earl and First Duke—Lionel Cranfield Sackville, 1688–1765—(*The Poems of Ambrose Philips*, ed. M. G. Segar, Percy Reprints, Blackwell, 1937)
13. From *Lapsus Calami and Other Verses*, first reprint of Collected Edition, 1898. These verses, unlike most of the others in this collection, are undated
16. Written autumn 1849 when Rossetti visited Paris and Belgium with Holman Hunt (*Works*, ed. W. M. Rossetti, 1911, 179 and Note)
17. Book VI, lines 79–88. *Aurora Leigh* dedicated to John Kenyon (see No. 78 and Note), was first published 1856
18. Waring, 'Mr. Alfred Dommett, C.M.G., author of "Ranolf and Amohia", full of descriptions of New Zealand scenery'
19. The Plaça Santiago, from *The Spanish Gypsy*, Book I. 'This work was originally written in the winter of 1864–5; after a visit to Spain in 1867 it was re-written and amplified.'—Authoress's Note, May 1868
20. Professor H. E. Rollins tells us that this poem was written 'to celebrate Wyatt's return to England from Spain in 1539', and quotes Drayton's opinion of it—'an excellent Epigram' (*Tottel's Miscellany, 1557–1587*, Harvard, II, 1939, 212)
21. Canto II, stanzas xiv, xviii–xxi. Canto II was published with Canto I 15 July 1819
22. Also from Canto II—stanzas xxiv–xxxii, xxxix, xlvi–vii, xlix–liii, lviii, lxiii, lxvi–vii, lxx–lxxiii, lxxv, lxxviii–ix, lxxxiv, lxxxvi, xcvi–viii, c, ciii

E. H. Coleridge refers to an article in *The Monthly Magazine*, August and September 1821, in which Byron's indebtedness to Sir G. Dazell's *Shipwrecks and Disasters at Sea*, 1812, is pointed out and where parallel passages are printed in full: he quotes Byron's Letter to John Murray, 23 August 1821—'With regard to the charges about the Shipwreck, I think I told you . . . years ago, that there was not a *single circumstance* of it *not* taken from *fact*; not, indeed, from any *single* shipwreck, but all from *actual* facts of different wrecks'

25. *Liberty*, Part IV, lines 297–308

26. *Julian and Maddalo: A Conversation* (composed autumn 1818, published post-humously 1824), lines 1–13, 63–92

27. *Rhymes on the Road extracted from the Journal of a member of the Poco-Curante Society*, Extract XII. The *Rhymes* were printed in 1812. The author's summary runs: *The English to be met with everywhere—Alps and Threadneedle Street—The Simplon and the Stocks—Blue Stockings amongst the Wahabees—Parasols and Pyramids—Mrs. Hopkins and the Wall of China*

28. From *Collected Poems*, 1933, 433–434. D. H. Lawrence writing from 32 Via dei Bardi, Florence, 17 September 1921, sent this poem with *Fish* and *Man and Bat* to his literary agent asking that it should be included in the section *Beasts* in *Birds, Beasts and Flowers*, published 1923, (*Letters* ed. A. Huxley, 1932, 524). Reprinted by courtesy of Mrs. Frieda Lawrence and Messrs. William Heinemann

30. IV, 44–76

31. From *Poems of Arthur Hugh Clough*, New and Revised Edition, 1888, 446–447

32. Included in *Verses on Various Occasions 1821–1862*, 1868. The circumstances and state of mind in which the lines were composed are well known from the *Apologia*. A footnote appended to line one reads: 'Of course this is the exclamation of one who was not in Catholic Communion'

33. This epistle, of which some twenty-six lines are not anthologized, appeared in Dodsley's *Collection of Poems*, vi, 1758. Thomas Lisle, who acted for a time as English Chaplain at Smyrna, was one of the brothers of the nine sisters for whom Pope wrote the *Inscription on a Grotto of Shells at Crux-Easton, the work of Nine Young Ladies* and *Verses occasioned by seeing a Grotto built by Nine Sisters*, also in this volume of Dodsley's *Collection*. W. P. Courtney informs us that Lord Carnarvon said in 1882 that the nine ladies used to pose in the grotto as the nine Muses, 'Pope being placed in the midst as Apollo'. (See *Dodsley's Collection of Poetry and Its Contributors*, 1910, 108–110)

34. Printed from MSS. by Myra Reynolds in *The Poems of Anne, Countess of Winchilsea*, Chicago, 1903

35. Appeared in *Timoleon*, first published 1891. Standard Edition, Constable, 1924, xvi, 284

36. IV, 237–250

37. The second epode relating the 'Progress of Poetry from Greece to Italy, and from Italy to England'. This ode, which Gray once called 'a high Pindarick upon stilts', was sent from Cambridge to his friend Thomas Wharton on 26 December 1754. First printed in 1757 by Horace Walpole's Press at Strawberry Hill

38. From *A Private Country*, 1943. The poem is dated 1940. Reprinted by courtesy of the Author and Faber & Faber, Ltd.

39. Included in *Verses on Several Occasions 1821–1862*, 1868. Dated 'The Oratory, 1856'

40. *The Strayed Reveller and Other Poems*. By A., 1849.

41. Cf. Byron, *Don Juan*, Canto V, stanza iii—'the very view which charmed the charming Mary Montagu'. She was writing from the Chiosk of the British Palace. According to Lord Wharncliffe's note (*Works*, 3rd edn., II, 1886, 449), these verses were sent by her from Constantinople to her uncle Fielding and 'by his (well intended) indiscretion shown about, copies taken, and at length miserably printed'. Lord Wharncliffe observes that 'the date, 1718, is clearly a mistake; for Lady Mary had returned to England before December of that year', that it must have been 1717, and that the poem first appeared in Anthony Hammond's Miscellany published in May 1720

42-43. For drafts of *Sailing to Byzantium* and *Byzantium* and suggestions about 'sources' see an article by Mr. A. Norman Jeffares in *The Review of English Studies* for January 1945. *Sailing to Byzantium*, written in 1926, was first published in *October Blast*, Cuala Press, June 1927, and then appeared as the opening poem of *The Tower* when it was published in February 1928. Yeats there gave one note—to Stanza IV: 'I have read somewhere that in the Emperor's palace at Byzantium was a tree made of gold and silver, and artificial birds that sang'. Mr. Joseph Hone in his biography of Yeats, 1942, 445, prints an account by Mr. G. R. Barnes of the alteration which Yeats made to the first line of the poem during a rehearsal for the programme called 'My Own Poetry' which was broadcast 3 July 1937 (introduced by Yeats, verse spoken by Mr. V. C. Clinton Baddeley and Margot Ruddock): 'When Baddeley read the first [two] lines . . . Yeats exclaimed "Stop! That is the worst bit of syntax I ever wrote", and promptly changed it to:

Old men should quit a country where the young. . . .'

Byzantium, written in 1930, was published in *Words for Music Perhaps*, Cuala Press, September 1932, and was then included in *The Winding Stair*, 1933, where Yeats, in the dedication to Edmund Dulac, tells of the 'return of life [after a long illness] as an impression of the uncontrollable energy and daring of the great creators', of how, during 'those exultant weeks', he wrote *Mad as the Mist and Snow* and *Words for Music Perhaps*. The dedication continues: 'Then ill again, I warmed myself back into life with *Byzantium* and *Veronica's Napkin*, looking for a theme that might befit my years'. See *Pages from a Diary written in 1930*, Cuala Press, 1944, 2, 3: '*Subject for a poem, April 30th*. . . . Describe Byzantium as it is in the system towards the end of the first Christian millennium. A walking mummy. Flames at the street corners where the soul is purified, birds of hammered gold singing in the golden trees, in the harbour, offering their backs to the waiting dead that they may carry them to paradise. . . . These subjects have been in my head for some time [i.e., Byzantium and 'Death of a friend' referred to earlier], especially the last'

From *Collected Poems* of W. B. Yeats, 1934, 217–218, 280–281. Reprinted by courtesy of Mrs. Yeats, Messrs. A. P. Watt & Son and Macmillan & Co.

44. Reprinted by courtesy of the Author and Faber & Faber, Ltd.

49. From *A Voice from the Nile and Other Poems* ed. Bertram Dobell, 1884. The poem is dated November 1881

50. Lx of *The Love Sonnets of Proteus* (first published 1880) from *The Poetical Works*, 1914, I, 94. Written on the way home to England early in the summer of 1876. 'It was customary then for tourists to go from Egypt to Syria by desert instead of by sea route. It was very unusual, however, for those unable to speak the language to travel without a dragoman. . . . The sole support of Blunt and Lady Anne were their camel-drivers, two Arab boys

from Sinai who knew almost nothing of the northern country. For several days they ran short of water, being totally ignorant of where the wells lay. . . .'—Edith Finch, *Wilfred Scawen Blunt 1840–1922*, 1938, 68–70. Reprinted by courtesy of the Author's Executors and Macmillan & Co.

51. Lines 106–128. 'Composed at Bishopsgate Heath, near Windsor Park, 1815 (autumn); published as the title-piece of a slender volume containing other poems. . . . London 1816 (March).'—Thomas Hutchinson, *Complete Poetical Works of Shelley*, Clarendon Press, 1904, 15

52. *The Modern Traveller. Verses by H. B. Pictures by B. T. B.* Published 1898. From Sections IV, V, VI. Reprinted by courtesy of the Author

53. From *The Wayzgoose: A South African Satire*, 1928. These are the first thirty-two lines. 'It [the Wayzgoose] appears to be a vast corroboree of journalists, and to judge from their own reports of it, it combines the functions of a bunfight, an Eisteddfod and an Olympic contest. . . .'—Author's remark. In another remark the Author gives an example of what he means in the lines

> A clime so prosperous both to men and kine
> That which were which a sage could scarce define

to which the footnote reads 'Example—"Wanted a good shorthorn typist". S.A. Paper.' Reprinted by courtesy of the Author and Jonathan Cape, Ltd.

54. From *The Fivefold Screen*, 1932, Section III, 'African Landscapes with Figures'. Reprinted by courtesy of the Author and The Hogarth Press, Ltd.

55. Writing to A. W. M. Baillie in 1864, the year in which *Enoch Arden* was published, Gerard Manley Hopkins (*Further Letters*, Oxford, 1938) gives the description of Enoch's tropical island as an instance of what he means by what he calls 'Parnassian', described on a different occasion as 'the language of poetry draping prose thought, a fine rhetoric'. He writes of this as a passage 'much quoted already and which will be no doubt often quoted. . . . In Parnassian pieces you feel that if you were the poet you could have gone on as he has done, you see yourself doing it, only with the difference that if you try you find you cannot write this Parnassian. . . . The glades being "like ways to Heaven" is, I think, a new thought, it is an inspiration. Not so the next line, that is pure Parnassian. If you examine it the words are choice and the description is beautiful and unexceptionable, but it does not *touch* you. The next is more Parnassian still. In the next lines I think the picture of the convolvuluses does touch; but only the picture: the words are Parnassian. It is a very good instance, for the lines are un-doubtedly beautiful, but yet I could scarcely point anywhere to anything which I could more clearly see myself writing *qua* Tennyson, than the words

> The glows
> And glories of the broad belt of the world

What Parnassian is you will now understand. . . .'
Earlier in the same letter he had written 'Do you know a horrible thing has happened to me. I have begun to *doubt* Tennyson'

56. From *Ha! Ha! Among the Trumpets. Poems in Transit*, 1945. The writer was killed in an accident while on active service in India, 1944. Reprinted by courtesy of Messrs. Allen & Unwin

57. III, 430–441

58. Bk. IV, lines 403–441. *The Fleece: A Poem in Four Books. By John Dyer, LL.B.* was first published 1757. The relevant part of Dyer's 'Argument' runs: 'Our woollen manufacturers known at Pekin, by the caravans from Russia—Description of that Journey'

59. From *The Gathering Storm*, first published September 1940. See the author's full note on the poem, pp. 67–70, from which excerpts only are given here.

'The grammar is meant to run through alternate lines; I thought this teasing trick gave an effect of completely disparate things going on side by side'

Red hills bleed naked into screes: 'The hills bleed in China because the trees have been cut down so that the red earth crumbles and washes away; it is an obvious symbol of disorder'

under-roaded: 'A bus is *under-roaded* when the road gives way under it and you spend hours digging in the mud and spreading branches'

the paddy fields are wings of bees: 'The paddy fields in hill country, arranged of course to make level patches to hold water, are extremely beautiful, look like microscopic photographs of bees' wings, and seem never to have been treated by all the long and great tradition of Far Eastern landscape painters'.

Reprinted by courtesy of the Author and Faber & Faber, Ltd.

60. This Chinese Eclogue is from *The Poetical Works of John Scott Esq.*, London, Buckland, 1782. The author annotates:

cotton harvests: The Chinese reduce the steep slopes of their hills into little terraces, on which they grow cotton, potatoes, etc. They plant the edges of their terraces with trees, which keep up the ground, and make a very fine appearance

rows of cypress: Their rice-grounds are separated by broad ditches, the sides of which are planted with cypresses

Vide Osbeck's *Voyage to China*

61. From *Selected Poems 1916–1936*, Oxford, 1939. Verses 5–9. This poem had earlier been published in the volume *The Dark Fire*, Sidgwick & Jackson, 1918. Reprinted by courtesy of the Author

62. From *Old Pastures*, New York, 1930. Reprinted by courtesy of the Author

63. *Summer*, lines 838–859

66. From *Journal of a West India Proprietor*, 1815. (The *Journal* was reprinted, ed. Mona Wilson, Routledge, 1929.) The poem (to which Lewis gave no title) is dated 10 December 1815, and the *Journal* continues at the conclusion of the poem: ' "And pray now do you mean to say that you really saw all this fine show?" Oh, yes, really, "in my mind's eye, Horatio," as Shakespeare says; or, if you like it better in Greek—"'Οσσόμενος Πάτερ' ἐσθλὸν ἐνὶ φρεσίν!" Odyssey, A'

Coleridge thought that in this 'delightful' book 'you have the man himself, and not an inconsiderable man,—certainly a much finer mind than I had supposed before from the perusal of his romances, &c. . . .' (*Table Talk*, 20 March 1834)

67. *The Indian Emperor, or The Conquest of Mexico by the Spaniards Being the Sequel of The Indian Queen* was published 1667. First performed in the spring of 1665 at the Theatre Royal. (See Hugh Macdonald, *Dryden Bibliography*, Oxford, 1939, 92, 93.) The lines anthologized are from Act I, Sc. i

68. These are stanzas 10–12. The speaker is the 'Youth from Georgia's Shore'. See notes given by the late Professor E. de Sélincourt, *Poetical Works of William Wordsworth*, II, Oxford, 1939, 509–510

'magnolia—*Magnolia grandiflora*'—W. W., 1800

'flowers that with one scarlet gleam. The splendid appearance of these scarlet flowers, which are scattered in such profusion over the hills in the southern parts of North America, is frequently mentioned by Bartram in his Travels.'—W. W., 1800.

Professor de Sélincourt also records Wordsworth's note dictated to Isabella Fenwick, 'Written in Germany 1799. Suggested by an account I had of a wanderer in Somersetshire', and tells us that it was E. H. Coleridge who first pointed out Wordsworth's general indebtedness in *Ruth* to Thomas Bartram's *Travels through North and South Carolina, Georgia, East and West Florida* . . . Philadelphia 1791, reprinted London 1792

69. From *Berkeley's Miscellany*, 1752

70. Reprinted by courtesy of the Author who has most kindly looked at a proof of the text given in the anthology

71. This is No. 80 of *100 Poems by Edward Thompson*, Oxford University Press, 1944. Reprinted by courtesy of the Author

72. From the group of Minor Poems—Landscapes, V—in *Collected Poems 1909-1935*, 1936. Reprinted by courtesy of the Author and Faber & Faber, Ltd.

73. These, the two last verses of *The Greenland Fishery*, 'In seventeen hundred and ninety-four, On March the twentieth day . . .', are taken from *A Garland of Country Song*, S. Baring Gould and H. Fleetwood Sheppard, 1895, No. XXVI, 56-7. Included in *The Oxford Book of Ballads*

74. *Poems by the Way* was published 1891. Morris went to Lithend on both his journeys to Iceland, in the summers of 1871 and 1873. (See J. W. Mackail's *Life*, 1899, Chapters VIII, IX.) Reprinted by courtesy of the Society of Antiquaries of London

75. From *Argalus and Parthenia* (first published 1629), the opening lines of The Second Part

76. From *Tales of the Hall*, Bk. IV.

77. LXIX–LXXV of 'Sed nos qui vivimus', one of the Sussex Pastorals. From *Poetical Works*, II, 1914. Written about 1888, published in *A New Pilgrimage and Other Poems*, Kegan Paul, 1889. (See Edith Finch, *Wilfred Scawen Blunt*, 1840–1922, 1938, 261.) Reprinted by courtesy of the Author's Executors and Macmillan & Co.

78. From *Poems: for the most part occasional*, 1838. John Kenyon was the friend of Coleridge, Southey, Landor, the Wordsworths, the Brownings and other writers. Dorothy Wordsworth writes of him and his brother, 25 August [1821] '. . . They live in all places, are at home everywhere and are most enchanting companions. . . .' (*The Letters of William and Dorothy Wordsworth*, The Later Years, I, Oxford, 1939, 1821–30, 45.) Wordsworth, in a letter to John Kenyon [June 1838], writes in acknowledging *Poems*, 'By the bye, Mrs. W. begs me to say that some passages of your Vol., the moonlight expecially, remind her of parts of my own work (still in MS) upon my early life. This is not the first instance where our wits have *jumped*, as great wits are apt to do.' *Ibid.*, II, 1831–40, 951

79. First published in *The Poems of John Ruskin*, ed. W. G. Collingwood, I, 1891, and written at the age of sixteen. The editor tells us that Miss R. was Mary Richardson, Ruskin's cousin and adopted sister, that Mary was Mary Stone, cook at Herne Hill, and Lucy, Lucy Tovey, the Ruskin's parlour maid from 1829–1875: he refers us to *Praeterita*, I Chaps. iv, vii, II Chap. vi. Reprinted by courtesy of Messrs. Allen & Unwin

80. From *A Diversity of Creatures*, 1917, 'In the Presence'. Reprinted by courtesy of Mrs. Bambridge and Macmillan & Co.

INDEX OF AUTHORS

Reference is to the Numbers of the poems, not to pages